A
CHRISTIAN
INTERPRETATION
OF
MARRIAGE

A
CHRISTIAN
INTERPRETATION
OF
MARRIAGE

by
HENRY A. BOWMAN

Philadelphia
THE WESTMINSTER PRESS

LIBRARY OF CONGRESS CATALOG CARD No. 59–5913

PRINTED IN THE UNITED STATES OF AMERICA

To My Wife and Son

*To the former with humble appreciation for a
 hope realized*
To the latter with sincere hope for a realization

CONTENTS

PREFACE

This book was written as an attempt to put into organized form the answers to myriad questions. Since 1934 I have been discussing marriage and preparation for marriage with people of various ages. This discussion has taken place in classes and in extracurricular, church, and community groups. In addition, during these years, I have talked in confidence with hundreds of individuals, married and unmarried, who have sought counseling aid in working through problems of marital adjustment or marriage preparation. Time and again I have been asked to discuss some aspect of the relationship between Christianity and marriage.

The reader will note that the title of this book is " *A* Christian Interpretation of Marriage." It is not " *The* Christian Interpretation of Marriage." Just which one is *the* Christian interpretation of marriage each individual must decide according to his own judgment and conscience. The book will, however, be read principally by Protestants; and the interpretation is Protestant.

Some readers may wonder how a professional sociologist, who seeks to be objective in his efforts to understand human society, can prepare a Christian interpretation of marriage. The reasons are three. In the first place, Christianity, with its various interpretations and applications, is part and parcel of the culture of this country. In the second place, when a teacher is made aware of a need as reflected in student questions, he is motivated to seek to meet that need. In the third place, a sociologist, although professionally he seeks objectivity, cannot as a human being in day-by-day activities and in wondering about the meaning of his own life be completely and exclusively objective. As an observer of life he may be objective. As a participator in life he cannot be. He must make choices and decisions. He does this by accepting the mores and folk-ways, by going along with common practices, by thinking through standards and establishing his own life philosophy, or by some other method or combination of methods. He cannot be entirely objective because his emotions, his relationships with other people, his welfare, and his happiness are involved. He is not a disembodied intellect. He must choose a way of life as a person. When an individual, no matter who he is, chooses a way of life, no matter what it is, from that point on he is biased. He need not lose his objectivity in social science, however, when, as a person, he orients himself toward ultimate reality. Objectivity in science, on the one hand, and agnosticism or atheism, on the other, are not synonymous. Science and religion, knowledge and faith, complement each other. They are not permanently antagonistic and conflicting opposites. So a scientist can be a Christian and find no inconsistency in that combination, because science and religion imply different universes of discourse.

All Biblical quotations to be found herein are from the Revised Standard Version. At the back of the book may be found New Testament verses pertinent to the topics discussed.

Many church groups plan an annual series of meetings focusing on preparation for marriage. Suggested plans for such meetings, together with questions for discussion and supplementary readings, may be found at the back of this book.

It would be impossible to specify all the persons to whom I am indebted in the preparation of this book. There have been too many. I am grateful to all who have written or spoken in the general area covered, to all who have wittingly or unwittingly suggested lines of thought and study, to all who have challenged me with questions, to all whose criticisms have motivated me to re-examine my own point of view. One person, however, I do want to specify. My indebtedness to my wife I cannot adequately put into words; but I can express my heartfelt appreciation for all that she has done and meant.

Henry A. Bowman

I THE NATURE OF SEX

Jesus' Attitude Toward Sex

Obviously, without sex and sexual differences there would be no marriage. Hence, it behooves us to seek an insight into a Christian attitude toward sex. Unfortunately, Jesus said relatively little about the subject. Paul said more, but much of what he said had a particular bearing on the situations in which the specific readers to whom his letters were addressed found themselves. Furthermore, as we shall see later, Paul's own status and his anticipation of the early return of Jesus colored some of his assertions about sex and marriage.

We get some side lights on Jesus' attitude through his few statements and also through his activities and his treatment of people. In so far as a judgment can accurately be made, his attitude seems to have been balanced, optimistic, healthy. One does not find in Jesus the distortions, inhibitions, fears, denials, or condemnations that are so frequently found in some of his present-day followers. Jesus was reared and educated as a Jew. In his day the Jews accepted the fact of sex as natural and desirable. Among them there was no Puritanical or ascetic punishing of the body for the hypothetical sake of the spirit, because they thought of body and spirit as one. There was no dualism in their philosophy. Jesus did, however, think in terms of use, motive, meaning, one's relationship to God and other persons.

11

Jesus attended the wedding at Cana. (John 2:1-2.) There is no suggestion that he was a relative of either bride or groom. Hence, he must have been invited because someone especially wanted him to be there, which implies at least that he approved of weddings. He never discriminated between the sexes; his relationships with both were based on an assumption of equality. At a time when Jews and Samaritans were involved in a situation in some ways similar to that of racial integration versus racial segregation in this country today, Jesus did not hesitate to talk with the Samaritan woman at the well (ch. 4:6-27). Both the woman herself and the disciples were astonished at what Jesus had done because of the Jewish-Samaritan antagonism: the fact that Jesus, a Jew, asked the Samaritan woman to do him a favor; the fact that Jesus, a man, talked with a woman about religion.

When the scribes and Pharisees brought to him the woman caught in the act of adultery (ch. 8:3-11), Jesus recognized that it was a trick to attempt to get him into trouble with the religious authorities; but he also showed deep understanding. He did not condone what she had done; neither did he condemn her. Technically, she could have been stoned to death in the street. Jesus had many women friends. Some accompanied him and the apostles as they went about preaching. (Luke 8:1-3.) It seems unlikely that a person whose attitude toward sex was anything but healthy and balanced would have behaved in this manner.

When Jesus said that for a man to look " at a woman lustfully " was equivalent to having committed adultery " in his heart " (Matt. 5:28), there is no implied condemnation of sex but rather a condemnation of the misuse of sex and an emphasis, as was common in Jesus' teaching, upon the motive behind the act. The verse in which this statement occurs follows another (v. 27) in which Jesus refers to one of the Ten Commandments, namely, " You shall not commit adultery." The Jews of Jesus' day were legalistically inclined to judge by overt behavior, while Jesus went beyond overt behavior to the motives underlying it. When he said that one was to pluck out an eye that was offensive or cut off a hand that was offensive (vs. 29-30), he was not condemning the very existence of eyes and hands, actually or figuratively, but rather, he was making a judgment of them according to the use to which they were put. It is highly likely that he would say a similar thing about sex.

Side Lights from Genesis

Oddly enough, we can get some side lights on a possible Christian attitude toward sex from the ancient book of Genesis, which was, of course, part of Jesus' "Bible," and from which, as we shall see later, he quoted in answer to a question about marriage. The book of Genesis was not written by one author. It is a compilation of stories, bits of history, oral records, allegories, and similar items selected by an editor from materials current in his time, some of which were already ancient. In the book are two accounts of the Creation. If, for the moment, we disregard details and discrepancies, we see in the first two chapters a great epic of creation painted, so to speak, with a wide brush. If the first portion of the book of Genesis were merely an ancient and primitive explanation of certain aspects of astronomy, geology, biology, it would have no place in our Bible. But it does have a place in our Bible because of what it tells us of the nature of man and his relationship to God.

In this great epic of creation the universe comes into being, plant and animal life is formed, and finally God makes mankind, in two sexes, but in ways different from the rest of the animals, for mankind is made "in the image of God" (Gen. 1:27). God is described as contemplating what he has created and deciding that it is good — both before and after the creation of the sexes.

At first Adam and Eve, who represent all of mankind and not merely two individuals, are completely innocent and sinless; and they live in a perfect environment. But then Eve is tempted to disobey God's commands and in turn tempts Adam to do likewise. From that point on, Adam and Eve are no longer innocent. They become ashamed of their bodies and their sexuality. But their offense is not sexual, as is often supposed; it is disobedience. They can differentiate between good and evil. They are sinful because they have rejected God and have separated themselves from him. This is the natural, congenital condition of man, namely, separation from God; hence, the need for redemption, for being brought back to God, and the need for a redeemer, a savior, a Christ.

Interpretations of the book of Genesis and the story of Adam and Eve range from insisting that it is word-for-word, line-for-line literal fact, to acceptance of it as entirely allegorical. However one may interpret it, it has something to say about the nature of sex and of man.

In the first place, man is unique in that he has free will, that is, he can make free judgments upon which to determine his actions. An animal can make simple choices, but it cannot make judgments. Secondly, man can relate himself to God. He can choose to accept or reject his creator. God is thought of as omnipotent. But man, to be man, must have the freedom to reject God if he so chooses. Otherwise man would be only another mammal, different in degree perhaps but not in any way in kind, quantitatively but not qualitatively, from the anthropoid apes. Thirdly, man has self-awareness. He knows what he does. He has the ability, at least to an appreciable degree, both to look within himself introspectively and to " stand off " from himself and look at himself, making himself simultaneously both subject and object. Fourthly, man knows what he ought to do. He formulates concepts of good and evil, moral and immoral, and imposes these concepts upon his own behavior. Fifthly, man reaches out beyond his immediate experience. For this reason man can participate with God in the ongoing process of creation. Man can take the raw materials of nature and out of them fashion works of art. Animals have hunger, but only man makes an art of cookery. Some animals have prehensile forepaws, but only man uses his hands to manipulate complicated tools or to produce beauty in painting or sculpture. Mammals have vocal cords and utter simple instinctive cries, but only man can utter a line of poetry or sing an aria. Animals have group living, but only man lives in terms of a moral structure. Animals have sex, bisexuality, sexual differences, but with animals sex is only procreative. Man alone can make sex creative. Only he can give it meaning. Only he can introduce a nonbiological, spiritual, interpersonal element into the sexual relationship, making sex a function of the whole personality. Only he can combine sex and love. Out of sex, rightly used, arise some of the most profound satisfactions, most meaningful human relationships, richest beauty of which man is capable. Out of sex misused arise some of the profoundest disappointments, most tragic interpersonal relationships, grossest ugliness known to man. Because man has freedom of will and of judgment, he can choose how he will use sex. He can choose to treat it casually, irresponsibly, immaturely, promiscuously. Or he can commit himself to a lifelong effort to establish sound and lasting monogamous marriage on a foundation of permanent and ever-growing love. If an individual raises his natural attributes, including sexuality, no higher than the animal level, he misses the point of being human.

THE FUNCTION OF SEX

This raises the question, What is the purpose of sex? Strictly speaking, perhaps, we should discuss it in terms of function rather than of purpose, since the true purpose of any part of creation is known only to God. But we are seeking to interpret man's relationship to God; and therefore, a discussion of purpose may be in order. Here, again, the ancient book of Genesis comes to our aid. It indicates that one purpose of sex is reproductive. But it also suggests that another purpose, by no means a secondary or subordinate one, is what might be termed communion or community. Sex is a God-ordained means of overcoming the essential loneliness of the individual human life. " Then the Lord God said, ' It is not good that the man should be alone.' " (Gen. 2:18.) " Therefore a man leaves his father and his mother and cleaves to his wife, and they become one flesh." (V. 24.) In this way, sex becomes not only a basis for interpersonal relationships but also a means of communication. Through sex and love in monogamous marriage, husband and wife enlarge one another's lives, each enabling the other, in a sense, to live doubly.

Because of sex, human life is bipolar instead of unipolar. Both male and female are focal points around which their common life revolves. Since this bipolar relationship is made necessary by the very nature of human life, it becomes inevitable that male and female should work out some sort of feasible mutual relationship. Christianity assumes that such a relationship can be raised to its highest point of development in permanent, monogamous marriage based on love of husband and wife for each other and their common orientation toward God.

Such a statement regarding monogamous marriage will, of course, be immediately challenged by some readers. They will insist that the values inherent in marriage are culturally relative and that therefore the above statement is dogmatic and absolute. Some will even affirm that there are no absolutes in human life. But to assume that all values are culturally relative may be to disregard the nature of man. All available evidence suggests that throughout all of known history and the world over, man is fundamentally the same. Must there not, then, be some values that represent the ultimate and are relative only to the basic nature of man? Christianity assumes that in the last analysis there is a way of life that is the best way, taking into account the nature of man, and that is the way of life taught and exemplified by Jesus.

If human sexuality, then, has a dual purpose, reproduction

and communion, and these purposes are on the same level of value, what about the problem of fulfilling one purpose only without the other? What about such a matter as contraception? The same creative process that imbued man with the capacity for procreation and the capacity for sexual responsiveness also imbued man with free will and the ability to apply judgment to his behavior. Hence, there is no more thwarting of a God-ordained process in the use of contraception than there is in putting sexual intercourse on a purely reproductive basis when there is no love between husband and wife or no sexual responsiveness on the part of the wife. In neither case is there any more thwarting of a God-ordained process than there is when man fails to apply his capacity for critical judgment, which is also God given, to the problems of human betterment. If, then, a couple decide to limit the number of their offspring in order to improve the upbringing of those they have, this is acceptable.

In this connection we must not be misled by the story of Onan, which some persons use as a Biblical argument against contraception. Er, Onan's elder brother, and the eldest son of Judah, died. "Then Judah said to Onan, 'Go in to your brother's wife, and perform the duty of a brother-in-law to her, and raise up offspring for your brother.' But Onan knew that the offspring would not be his; so when he went into his brother's wife he spilled the semen on the ground, lest he should give offspring to his brother. And what he did was displeasing in the sight of the Lord, and he slew him also." (Gen. 38:8-10.)

What was "displeasing in the sight of the Lord" was not the fact that Onan practiced a simple form of contraception. It was Onan's refusal to fulfill the law regarding levirate marriage. "If brothers dwell together, and one of them dies and has no son, the wife of the dead shall not be married outside the family to a stranger; her husband's brother shall go in to her, and take her as his wife, and perform the duty of a husband's brother to her. And the first son whom she bears shall succeed to the name of the brother who is dead, that his name may not be blotted out of Israel." (Deut. 25:5-6.) One of the most important things in a man's life was the securing of a male heir. Therefore, for a man to refuse to become a levir was a serious offense strongly disapproved by public opinion. In fact, the law provided that, if a man refused to do his duty, the brother's wife should publicly spit in his face. (Vs. 7-10.)

Man is also unique in that he can conceive of the future, and can relate the present to the future, even to the eternal. Therefore, man is the only creature that can have marriage. Animals may have lifelong mating; but this is instinctive. It involves no commitment. Because they have no culture and live only in the present, animals can have no marriage. Marriage does involve commitment.

II THE NATURE OF MARRIAGE

CHRISTIAN MARRIAGE BEGINS WITH FAITH

There is a not uncommon assumption to the effect that Christian marriage is essentially ethical marriage, that is, that a couple have a Christian marriage if they live together with at least a minimum of respect, love, and decency. This is a reflection of the broader assumption that Christianity itself is largely a system of ethics — love your neighbor as yourself; treat others as you would have them treat you; exhibit commonly approved virtues; do this and refrain from doing that; help to establish the perfect society; live the good life. Admittedly, a system of ethics is an integral part of the Christian point of view. But if Christianity is no more than that, there is no such thing as the Christian religion. By the same token, a Christian marriage must be more than an ethical marriage. It must also, perhaps we should say fundamentally, be a religious marriage. But, except in so far as there are problems in interfaith marriage, or there is a problem of religious education of children, or a couple must decide between a civil and a church wedding ceremony, how can a marriage be religious? For that matter, what makes anything religious as distinguished from nonreligious?

In this book we shall use the terms "religion" and "religious" within the framework of American culture, not in the broader anthropological framework within which their possible definitions would be subject to greater variation and wider implication. As we shall use the terms, therefore, they imply a belief in God — an assumption, a premise, an act of faith to the effect that God exists — and what man does about or because of that belief. From this primary element of faith emerge secondary elements of faith which are meaningless without the primary element and which, in their turn, become acceptable in the light of the primary element upon which they depend.

In this era of emphasis upon scientific method and research, upon verifiability, upon empirical data, there is a certain prestige attributed to knowing and a certain magnanimous tolerance of ignorance. To say "I know" and to be able to prove it gives one status. To say "I don't know" indicates one's humility in the confrontation of the still-to-be-known and one's reliance upon science though it may be incomplete and limited. But to set up another alternative and say "I believe" is for many folks anathema.

Yet faith represents a valid approach to reality. It is a function of the same mind as that of which knowledge is a function. While faith may not have the same advantages in utilizing the products of the senses as does knowledge, neither is it limited by the limitations of the senses as is knowledge. Besides, faith is not something that operates only in relation to things religious. Before an individual can know anything he must assume that he exists, that his mind is such that it can know, that it can recognize truth, that his observations can represent accurate reflections of reality, that he can communicate what he has observed. All of these are acts of faith. We ordinarily assume that they all are valid. It is equally valid to assume that the human mind has the capacity to approach God through faith. Faith, then, is not equivalent to wild imagination or wishful thinking, or blind, uncritical acceptance of the improbable. It is a considered reaction of the human mind to the evidence with which it is confronted, plus the ability to go beyond immediate evidence in a manner not entirely dissimilar to that in which immediate evidence is transcended in the formulation of concepts, abstractions, hypotheses, formulae, in prediction, in asserting ignorance. How can a man, except through making an assumption that carries him beyond his observations and is, therefore, an act of faith, say, "I know that there are things that I do not know"? Man is handicapped in his observations because he himself is an integral part of the universe he seeks to understand. For this reason, all his knowledge is relative to his own capacity for knowing. Being aware of this relativity, he assumes an absolute, namely, God.

Granted, then, the faith that God exists, questions arise as to his attributes and his relation to man. Christianity answers these questions by describing God as living and active in the universe, thus suggesting that the creative process is still going on; as loving and just, and thus concerned about man; as approachable by and accessible to man, thus suggesting the validity of worship and prayer; as knowable to man through numerous channels but especially through his impact upon human life and particularly through the life of Jesus Christ.

Christian marriage begins, then, not with a system of ethics, but with faith — faith in the existence of God, confidence in God's attributes, assurance of the manifestation of God in Jesus Christ. Perhaps we should say that Christian marriage begins with faith plus awareness plus intent. Faith in God's existence is fundamental, but it is the beginning only. There must also be an awareness of God's presence, and an intent on the part of the couple to relate their marriage to God as they are aware of him, so that in so far as their abilities permit they make their marriage an expression of their relationship to God. As in any marriage the Christian husband and wife naturally have a deeply meaningful relationship to each other. But they also recognize their own incompleteness, the unavoidability of their living each in his own private world. To a degree they transcend this incompleteness, this inevitable separateness, by a common orientation toward God.

This orientation is implied in the opening statement of the Christian wedding ceremony: "Dearly beloved, we are gathered here in the sight of God" or "in the presence of God." God is omnipresent. He is no more in one place than in any other. The emphasis in this statement, therefore, is not upon "*here*," but rather upon "*in the sight* [or *presence*] *of God.*" The statement reminds the couple that what they are about to do is God-related. It is not merely a matter of personal choice, legal sanction, or societal significance. It is first and primarily a matter of ultimate orientation, an expression of highest intention, an awareness of essential meaning. The couple's bodies will permit them to establish a sexual, a procreative relationship. Their God-centered orientation will permit them to establish a spiritual, a creative relationship.

CHRISTIANITY'S CONTRIBUTION TO MARRIAGE

Whatever contribution Christianity makes to marriage must, of course, come through the behavior of husband and wife, separately or jointly. There is no magic, no ectoplasmic presence, no voice from heaven, no oracle to communicate the supernatural. There is only faith, commitment, love, self-discipline, ego surrender — for none of which there is an adequate substitute, and all of which are hard to achieve. In addition, of course, the Christian believes there is grace, the unearned increment. Some of the things the Christian is impelled to do he does not feel competent to do through his own ability. But he believes that God is accessible to him both in the sense that he can approach God through prayer and in the sense that through God's assistance he may accomplish things he could never accomplish on the basis of his own resources alone. This is part of the Christian's interpretation of God as living and active, both in the universe at large and in human life. (Items in the rest of this chapter have been adapted from the author's *Marriage for Moderns*, 3d ed., McGraw-Hill Book Co., Inc., 1954.)

Christianity provides life with its most far-reaching, most timeless perspective. It places human life in a cosmic frame of reference. It thus enables man to rise above his earth-bound, time-bound limitations. As man relates himself to the infinite and the eternal he becomes less threatened by the ups and downs of current events, by the confusion of temporal affairs, by the vicissitudes of life, by ephemeral and counterfeit values. Thus man may achieve spiritual triumph over failure. He may exhibit enduring patience in the face of seemingly overwhelming problems. He may sustain hope when circumstances appear hopeless. In short, man may achieve poise through faith.

This perspective, this frame of reference, gives validity to idealism. An individual may set up objectives unattainable in themselves but of such nature that, in a sense, they may be achieved through the very process of striving for them. This is applicable to the ultimate goals in life, not to such things as vocational ambition. "You, therefore, must be perfect," said Jesus. (Matt. 5:48.) That is, the Christian sets his expectations for himself at infinity. He thinks in terms of the ultimate, the absolute, endless and unlimited personal growth, what ought to be. In the light of his expectations and his demands upon himself, his achievements seem meager indeed. He never seems able to lift himself by his bootstraps. Try as he will, he cannot seem to improve, for he is constantly falling short here or making mistakes there. True, as he looks back on what he was yesterday, he may honestly feel that in a particular respect he is better today. But he keeps reminding himself of other respects in which he is not what he should be. In a figurative way he faces a problem that would be faced by an interplanetary traveler. If we assume that the universe is infinite, then such a traveler might measure how far he had moved from Earth. But no matter how far he had moved from Earth, no matter how long he traveled, he would be no closer to infinity than when he started.

This sets up what might be termed the Christian's dilemma. He is called upon to strive for a perfection that he knows in advance he can never achieve. But the inevitability of his failure is in no way to reduce the ardor of his striving. He continuously falls short of the ideal. " I do not understand my own actions," said Paul. " For I do not do what I want, but I do the very thing I hate." (Rom. 7:15.) As phrased in the General Confession in the Protestant Episcopal *Book of Common Prayer* this becomes: " We have erred, and strayed from thy ways like lost sheep. We have followed too much the devices and desires of our own hearts. We have offended against thy holy laws. We have left undone those things which we ought to have done; and we have done those things which we ought not to have done; and there is no health in us."

Unless something were added, such a point of view would lead to complete and ultimate frustration and hopelessness. But for the Christian two important things are added. One is the concept of the importance of commitment. The central goal to which an individual has committed himself, the central focus of his life, his basic orientation, is of greater concern than what he has achieved. Better to feel zero attainment while seeking unsuccessfully to reach the highest goal than to feel greater attainment while reaching toward a lesser goal. " Seek first his kingdom and his righteousness," said Jesus. (Matt. 6:33.)

The other thing that is added is the Christian's assurance that the love of God is infinite and is extended to both the deserving and the undeserving. Such love cannot be purchased. It cannot be earned. The individual cannot do anything to make himself deserving of it. It is a gift. Hence, the truly repentant can be assured of forgiveness, not because he deserves it, but because God is merciful. Those who keep striving for the unattainable have a sense of security, not because of what they have achieved, but because of what they are seeking to achieve. This gives rise to the concept of salvation by faith, not by works. Acceptance of this concept can give the Christian a peace of mind, " the peace of God, which passes all understanding." Then the Christian continues to strive for the perfect ideal, not in order to make God love him, but because God loves him and he loves God and is grateful to God. All that he does he counts as insignificant in comparison to what he receives. Hence, Christianity is a religion of worship and gratitude, not a religion of fear and demand.

With commitment to the Christian ideal goes ego surrender. With ego surrender goes a reduction in the number and types of things for which some persons strive or which constitute a threat to the individual or his marriage.

A parallel to the distinction between the *in order to* and the *because of* approach to God's love and the striving for the Christian ideal may be found in the role played by love in marriage. To be loved by another person is one of the greatest privileges in life. Upon what basis shall I assume that I can be, or will be, loved by my spouse? Is it because I am so lovable? If I assume that I should be loved because I am so lovable, I exhibit such egotism that I would immediately be unlovable. Is it because I do so much for that spouse? If I assume this, then it is logical to assume that the more I do the more I ought to be loved. The only basis upon which I may safely assume that I will be loved by my spouse is that of assuming that that person is sufficiently loving to love even me because I am I, undeserving as I may be. Then I do things selflessly for that person, not in order to make that person love me, but because that person loves me and I love that person. This works both ways in a successful marriage. The result is that each spouse makes a continuous and growing contribution to the happiness of the other person without expectation of return except such return as is to be found in the joy of giving.

Christianity attributes to each individual a fundamental worth, a core of importance, that demands respect in appraisal of him and consideration in action toward him, no matter what, in a more specific sense, he may be or do. It does this because of the individual's humanness, the fact that being human he is a child of God. Under no circumstances is he ever to be treated as if he were an animal or a thing. Being human, he needs love. In fact, he needs love most when he is most unlovable.

Christianity places primary emphasis upon each individual as a person. The things connected with him are of no consequence. It suggests that there is about each personality something indestructible, and therefore eternal. More important than a person's behavior are his attitudes and motives. Hence, he may be judged separate from his acts. This does not imply that his acts are unimportant, but only that they are not the final basis for appraisal. Unless he has proof to the contrary, a Christian is inclined to assume that another person's motives are good. At best, he is hesitant about judging another's motives.

Of all possible motives, Christianity maintains that the most important one, the one giving rise to most effective action toward human betterment, the one that contributes most profoundly to deeply satisfying life experience, is love. This love is other-person-centered. It is outgoing and results in forgetfulness of self. It leads to giving for the sake of the well-being of another, rather than the expectation of return. It is expressed through service to others. It is never diverted to the exploitation of others. It lies at the root of the most profound and meaningful sharing of which human personality is capable. Such love dissolves the barriers between the self and the other-than-self. It enables the individual to identify himself with the totality of human life. Such an identification does not destroy self. It extends self into a new dimension.

Christianity gives rise to dynamic good will, a constructive, confident attitude toward the potentialities for development to be found in each person. This is different from what may be termed passive good will, a tolerant acceptance of the continued presence and essential variability of human beings. Such dynamic good will enables a person confidently to appraise other individuals in terms of their highest possibilities rather than only in terms of their achievements. Dynamic good will can also influence an individual's development in a direction defined in part by a person who has confidence in him.

While Christianity attributes to each human being a fundamental dignity and worth, it also introduces a seeming incongruity in this connection. It suggests that the Christian judge himself more harshly than he judges others. When he thinks of others and their shortcomings, he thinks in terms of understanding and forgiveness, of patience and generosity. But when he thinks of himself, he thinks in terms of responsibility, of the unattainable ideal far from which he finds himself in spite of his efforts. While he forgives others for their shortcomings, he does not forgive his own. He does not expect in others what he demands in himself. He forgives in others what he does not excuse in himself.

At a time when there is widespread and common emphasis upon quantitative evaluation — frequency curves, measurement, numerical analysis, the counting of things to establish their importance — Christianity suggests qualitative evaluation. It suggests that there are some things of such nature that one occurrence is one too many. This Christianity accomplishes in part by establishing principle, truth, God-relatedness, rather than frequency of occurrence as the valid basis for judgment. It is not how often an individual does a certain thing that matters, but rather what he does and why he does it. "Whoever causes one of these little ones who believe in me to sin, it would be better for him to have a great millstone fastened round his neck and to be drowned in the depth of the sea," said Jesus. (Matt. 18:6.) Here and elsewhere there is the implication that an act may almost constitute an absolute; to commit it once is as bad as to repeat it.

In another way Christianity suggests qualitative rather than quantitative evaluation. In emphasizing the importance of each person's doing his best with the capacities at his disposal and the importance of working together for common ends, it tends to eliminate competition. The point is to do all that one can, not just to do more than someone else.

Christianity contributes to consistency of behavior both because it suggests the integration of personality around basic values and also because it affects decision-making. Once an individual has committed himself to the Christian point of view, once he has made the major decision, then many other decisions become of lesser importance. If an individual had to make a judgment concerning his over-all goal every time he had to make a decision, every decision would seem of major proportions. If he makes decisions that are inconsistent, he may precipitate conflict within himself. If, on the other hand, he commits himself once and for all to a central purpose, conflict is reduced and consistency is promoted.

THE CULTURAL FRAMEWORK OF MARRIAGE

Christian marriage though basically religious is not exclusively religious. It occurs within a cultural framework and according to legal definitions. This fact, too, is referred to in the wedding ceremony in such statements as "in the face of this company" and "If any man can show just cause, why they may not lawfully be joined together, let him now speak, or else hereafter forever hold his peace." The societal aspects of marriage are also indicated by the requirement of a license, an officiant (except for some groups), and witnesses. The implication is that marriage is a relationship between two persons and may through them be related to God, who originally created the two sexes, but that marriage is also a matter of concern for the state. This is true in part because a man and a woman are not entirely separate, discrete, unattached individuals. They are in a sense the bridge between families — the parental families on the one hand, the couple's own family and later their children's new families on the other. It is families, not separate isolated individual units, that constitute society.

III PREMARITAL SEXUAL RELATIONS

IS THE PROBLEM NEW?

Attitudes toward premarital sexual intercourse run the gamut from absolute and complete condemnation, on the one hand, to recommending that all restrictions be removed, on the other. Even "experts" disagree. One wonders what lies behind these various attitudes. One is driven to the conclusion that there is a jumble of rationalizing of wants into "needs," of immature thinking, of reliance upon tradition, of exploitation, of rationalizing of engagements ("We're going to get married anyway, so why wait?"), of information and misinformation, of truths and half-truths, of carefully thought out values and a disregard of values.

To what degree the problem of premarital sexual intercourse, as we are aware of it today, is new and how frequently such intercourse occurs are questions still to be answered. There is some useful evidence, but it is not conclusive. What evidence there is, suggests that the frequency is higher than the most optimistic persons have been inclined to assume, but perhaps not so high as the most pessimistic have been inclined to insist. The problem per se is not new. It is more openly discussed than it used to be, and this may give a partial illusion of newness. There is evidence to suggest that there has been some change with respect to the women involved. Men, in this country, have traditionally had more sexual freedom than have women. Generalizing broadly, in earlier times there was some tendency for men's sexual freedom to be exercised with women who belonged to a group from which the men did not choose their wives. Now there is a greater tendency for the women to belong to the group from which the men choose their wives. Studies show that many of these women are engaged to the men with whom the intercourse occurs.

BASIS FOR APPRAISAL

In order to rest on a Christian base, whatever appraisal is made regarding premarital sexual intercourse, in the case of an individual or a couple, must involve a set of values. But it must also be particularized: When did this happen? How often? At what age? With whom? Why? What were the motives behind it? What has it done to the persons involved? Is it all in the past? Is it current? Is it likely to be repeated? What is the person's or couple's attitude toward it?

We do this when we make an appraisal of other types of behavior, for example, of honesty versus dishonesty. On the one hand, we can think of honesty as a value and therefore deplore any act of dishonesty. On the other hand, when an individual has been dishonest, we tend to particularize. Did he steal once when he was a child or does he regularly engage in theft? When he stole, was it something like jumping a fence and taking some apples, or did he enter someone's home and take money? Is the dishonesty all past or is it likely to be repeated? What is the individual's present attitude toward honesty? The law and the courts take such factors into consideration with regard to human behavior. It is not expecting too much to expect Christians to do so.

In appraising premarital sexual intercourse, there is another factor that must be taken into consideration. Most young people want to marry someday and they want their marriage to be happy and successful. They do not expect to remain celibate for life. Therefore, premarital sexual intercourse must be evaluated in the light of the goal of marriage that young people set for themselves. Such intercourse cannot be treated as if it were an isolated phenomenon, disconnected from the rest of life. Such questions as the following become especially pertinent: How is premarital sexual experience related to marriage? Does it contribute anything or does it detract something? Is such experience good or poor preparation for marriage? Is it necessary preparation for marriage? What is learned by the individuals involved? Is what is learned useful or is it something that will have to be unlearned before the couple can work out a satisfactory sexual relationship in marriage?

With regard to the matter of a successful sexual adjustment in marriage, one frequently hears this argument: If sex in marriage is so important, does it not make sense to test each other out before the wedding? Such a suggestion might make sense if it were feasible. A couple who have premarital sexual intercourse and discover thereby that the girl is responsive admittedly have learned something. But suppose that the girl is not responsive, as is so often the case. What have they learned? Will they assume that they should not marry? Will they solve the problem or accentuate it?

A wiser approach to this problem is to assume that, granting no anatomical complications and no extreme inhibitions or fears, which could in most cases be ascertained through discussion, a normally healthy young couple who are in love and have a will to succeed can work out a satisfactory sexual adjustment in marriage. They do not need to think in terms of testing each other. They think in terms of building something together. They accept each other on faith just as they do with regard to possible future parenthood. This sort of faith is suggested in the wedding ceremony.

Another argument not infrequently put forward by men is that sexual continence is damaging to males. The fact is that although such sexual restraint may be difficult and even uncomfortable, it is in no way damaging, especially when the individual's objective is marriage rather than merely restraint per se. Self-discipline has an important place in life even today when it has lost some of its popularity. Certainly there are times other than before the wedding when a man may be expected to exercise self-discipline relative to sex, for example, when his wife is ill or pregnant, when she is away from home, when he is separated from her during military service. Intelligent self-discipline is not something new to and untried by a Christian. He exercises it in many aspects of life, especially as he relates his behavior to his ultimate goals, to the kind of person he wants to become, to his understanding of the basic nature of man, to his relationship with other persons. There is no place in Jesus' philosophy of life for a path of least resistance, a cream-puff and marshmallow approach to behavior. "If any man would come after me," said Jesus, "let him deny himself and take up his cross and follow me." (Matt. 16: 24.) This injunction can be and has been used as one of the bases for the most extreme forms of asceticism. But that was not what Jesus was implying. He was implying the path of ego surrender as the most valid road to a full Christian life, an intelligent subordination of the less consequential and immediate to the ultimately meaningful.

BASIS FOR SOLUTION

Premarital sexual intercourse is a personal problem, a social problem, a philosophical problem, and a moral problem, the last because it is unavoidably related to the structure and welfare of society. In seeking a solution to this problem, certain questions must somehow be answered.

How does, or how should, an individual decide which societal practices and changes to approve and accept, which to reject, resist, or deplore? To what degree should a person be influenced by changing societal norms? What is a societal norm — what is done by the majority, what is expected, what is considered desirable, what is tolerated? For example, how does or how should an individual decide whether or not to go along with a change in fashion, to accept or resist the present-day trend in married women's wage-earning, to approve or deplore racial integration, to accept or reject premarital sexual relations? Each individual has somehow on some basis to make a decision. Any one or more of the following may be included in that basis of decision: the assumption that the new is better than the old; the assumption that the old is better than the new; what is thought to be best for self; what is thought to be best for others; what is considered to be best for all in the " long run "; doing uncritically " what everybody's doing "; a weighing of values; a relating of choices to ideals; a relating of decisions to moral precepts; a relating of decisions to religion, that is, the individual's relationship to God. Christianity suggests that if the individual made his decision on the basis of his relationship to God and to the values and ideals promulgated by and personified in Jesus, the rest of the items in this list would be taken care of. To some things, such as a minor change in fashion, Christianity would not apply. But in the major issues of life, it usually has a bearing.

There is no necessary relationship between what is and what ought to be. The former is a matter of fact. The latter is a matter of value-oriented judgment. In some instances, of course, what is and what ought to be coincide. In other instances they are at variance. For example, there is a reasonable degree of correlation between what is and what we think ought to be with regard to free enterprise in this country, freedom of speech and worship, the protection of bank deposits. But what about the discrepancy between what is and what ought to be with regard to traffic safety, honesty, courtesy, marital success, personal and social hygiene, the profession and the behavior of some Christians? Into which category is premarital sexual intercourse to be put, and on what basis? Are we to conclude that general practice is to dictate norms? Or are we to assume that even if general practice approached 100 per cent, that would still not necessarily determine what ought to be? Do norms always have to grow out of behavior or can ideals be applied to behavior? Christianity asserts the latter.

On what basis is a line to be drawn between individual freedom and societal welfare? Suppose a man drives on the open highway at night with his wife and small children in the car and at the rate of 100 miles per hour. Has he committed an immoral act? It may be assumed that he is jeopardizing the safety of his family and that of other drivers. Must judgment be suspended until we can ascertain whether he has an accident and someone is killed? Or can judgment be made on the basis of the possible and potential danger involved? Suppose that in a room full of people an individual draws a gun and starts firing at random. Can a judgment as to whether or not he should be allowed such freedom be made before anyone is shot? Or must we wait to make a judgment until we see whether anyone gets shot? It seems clear that the possible and potential results of an act considered in prospect, as well as the actual results considered in retrospect, must be taken into consideration. One reason for this is that the potentialities of the act are related to our estimate of the value of human life and personality. Since Christianity makes human life and personality second in importance only to God, it suggests bringing judgment to bear upon the potentialities of a particular act even before such an act is committed. Since there is as yet no perfect, 100 per cent foolproof contraception, each act of premarital intercourse, with a few exceptions in cases of sterility, is potentially procreative. This means that the couple who have the intercourse are not the only ones to be considered. There is the possible third person, the child. Any act that contains within itself the possibility of being detrimental to another person is, in the Christian philosophy, disapproved.

Let us look at this matter of risk of pregnancy from another angle, still keeping in mind the Christian philosophy mentioned above. If an individual wants to play " Russian roulette " with the gun pointed at his own head, that is one problem. But if he wants to play " Russian roulette " with the gun pointed at someone else's head, that is quite another thing. In premarital sexual intercourse the woman does not assume the entire risk. But she does assume the greater risk. Yet much premarital intercourse occurs on masculine initiative. Who, then, plays " Russian roulette " with the gun pointed at whose head? Again Christianity declares its disapproval of any act through which one individual jeopardizes another individual's welfare for selfish purposes.

But suppose there were perfect, 100 per cent foolproof contraception so that the risk of pregnancy were entirely removed. Would this make any difference in the appraisal of premarital intercourse? Is there anything involved in this appraisal besides fear of pregnancy? If so, what? On numerous occasions the author has suggested to his classes that they imagine a hypothetical situation. As suggested above, perfect contraception is to be assumed. Then, under such circumstances, would members of the class approve or disapprove of their " boy friends " or " girl friends," fiancés or fiancées, having sexual relations with someone else? Most of them express strong and immediate disapproval. They go even farther than a disapproval of sexual relations. They disapprove also of such persons being affectionate with someone else. Some even go so far as to object to the other person's dating someone else during an extended separation. It is clear that they think in terms of values other than the prevention of pregnancy.

Part of this reluctance to share each other with other persons is no doubt an expression of possessiveness and insecurity. But part of it also is an indication of the common tendency to think about such relationships in terms of exclusiveness, the kind of exclusiveness that reaches its highest point in permanent monogamous marriage. This exclusiveness is implied in the wedding ceremony: " forsaking all others, keep thee only unto him [or her] " and " to have and to hold from this day forward." Such exclusiveness is brought to its highest point in marriage. It is brought to a sharp focus of intent in the wedding. But it does not begin with the wedding. It begins with each individual's capacity or readiness for exclusiveness that he brings to the wedding. This, in turn, would depend upon the degree to which an individual had "shared" himself sexually before the wedding. Such sharing would depend partly upon sexual activity, partly upon the attitudes underlying such activity at the time it occurred, and the change in them since. Let us consider, for example, three hypothetical unmarried persons. The first has maintained a standard of premarital chastity. The second had premarital intercourse a few times in his earlier years, but in his late teens and early twenties his attitudes changed and he maintained a standard of chastity. The third started in his early teens and frequently had premarital sexual intercourse from that time until his wedding, even having it with someone other than his fiancée during the engagement. Do these three hypothetical persons approach the wedding with the same capacity for sexual exclusiveness in marriage? If we think not only in terms of the individual's own attitudes but also in terms of the attitudes of his marriage partner toward his earlier sexual partners, the answer to this question must be in the negative.

This is not to be interpreted as a condemnatory judgment upon anyone. It is intended as a recognition of fact. Jesus abhorred condemnatory judgments. More than once he indicated that there was no one who himself was good enough in his own life so to condemn another person. Jesus also taught the principles of forgiveness and the second chance. In his thinking, anyone who sincerely wanted to turn a corner in his life and start again on a new path with a new intention had the inherent right, the God-given privilege, to do so. But this does not change the reality of the fact that everything an individual does becomes a permanent part of his biography. It is one thing to forgive what a person has done, whether that forgiveness comes from God or man. It is another to declare that forgiveness erases the fact that he did it.

Another tenet of Christian teaching that has a bearing on this matter of premarital sexual intercourse and one that was mentioned earlier in another connection is this: a human being, no matter who or what he may be, is always to be treated as a person, never as a thing. He is never to be exploited. With a person an individual can establish meaningful interpersonal relationships. A thing is to be used. How it is used is of no consequence so far as the thing itself is concerned. A thing is not something to be loved, to be respected. Much premarital intercourse involves one individual's using another as if that other were a thing to be appropriated for selfish satisfaction. This is not always one-sided, as some persons assume. It is not always the man who uses the woman, although this is common enough. Certainly there are cases in which the woman uses the man as if he were a thing. She may do this by encouraging or permitting sexual intercourse for material gain, for attention, in order to bind him to her, by deliberately playing upon his vulnerability to physical appeal. When she does one of the above, she is also acting as if she considered herself a thing.

Couples in Love

Some of these items do not apply to a couple who are sincerely in love, perhaps engaged, and are in the process of establishing an enduring interpersonal relationship. If they have premarital intercourse, they may not actually be using each other as things. They may even have a sense of assurance that if pregnancy occurs they will marry a bit sooner since they plan to marry eventually anyway. What about them? There are for them some pertinent practical questions. Studies indicate that approximately one fourth to one third of engaged couples break their engagements before each marries someone else. How can a particular couple be sure they will marry?

Counseling experience and observation suggest that in some cases in which a couple marry or marry earlier than they planned in order to camouflage a premarital pregnancy, that fact complicates marital adjustment, upsets plans for educational or occupational training, strains the relationship between the couple and their parental families. This is not the result in all cases. But how can a particular couple be certain of the prediction in their own case? Again in counseling, the author has talked with young couples who had premarital intercourse as what to them seemed an expression of love, only to find that after the act they felt disappointment and suspicion. First sexual intercourse is more like a milestone than a casual incident in many a person's life. How can anyone be sure what his attitudes will be after such an experience?

Is it consistent, even mature, for an individual to seek privilege without first accepting responsibility for the consequences of such privilege? In the Christian wedding ceremony the couple take a stand on responsibility, not casually, not only verbally, but " in the sight of God, and in the face of this company." Granted that in these days they have no complete assurance that their marriage will be permanent, at least they have done what the church and society expect and as much as they can. They have indicated their intent.

Marriage Rests on a System of Values

In the last analysis, if, either individually or as a people, we want to solve the problem of premarital sexual relations, we shall have to recognize that the "solutions" employed up to this point have not been solutions at all. Tradition uncritically accepted, letting common practice dictate the standard, evasion, fear of pregnancy, threat of disapproval, rationalization of pleasure, have thus far left much to be desired. There seems to be no alternative to the Christian imperative to put first things first.

Many present-day Americans are striving to work out a type of marriage that, with regard to some of its elements, is new in history. It is new in its emphasis upon interpersonal relationships, upon personal satisfaction. It rests upon the assumption that love is its most appropriate cornerstone. It entails an awareness of the importance of mutuality, an unfettered association of two complementary equals whose sharing of a common life is as full and as nearly complete as the capabilities and limitations of human personality permit. It includes an expectation of sexual exclusiveness. Such marriage is inextricably bound up with idealism, with concepts of what makes life meaningful, what is worth striving for. Marriage thus becomes one of life's major goals. It becomes a way of life, not merely a part of life. It presents possibilities for personality development and fulfillment second to none. It rests upon a system of values. The values in this system are integrated. They are not just a helter-skelter conglomeration. If one part of the structure is disturbed, the entire structure suffers. Hence, to preserve the structure, each value in it must be preserved.

More than any other type of marriage known, this kind approaches the Christian ideal and at least potentially incorporates within itself the attitudes and principles taught and exemplified by Jesus. Individually and collectively, then, we shall have to decide whether this is the kind of marriage we want. If it is, then we shall have to do whatever is necessary to achieve it. In doing so, the least that might be expected is consistency. If this kind of marriage is important to us, then each element in it is important. We cannot treat one element as if it were essential, while we treat another casually. If an individual wants sound, successful, meaningful, Christian marriage, the pattern of values that characterizes that individual's life must be sound and consistent. A casual, pleasure-seeking, irresponsible approach to sex as if it were unrelated to the rest of life, either before marriage or in marriage, introduces an element of inconsistency into the over-all structure. Casual sexual contact between temporary partners for pleasure alone belies the potentialities of sex as a means of communication, as a way of establishing community. Such community can be established only as sex is combined with love. Only through such a combination can husband and wife become "one flesh."

Admittedly, the above is a definition of a lofty ideal, perhaps unattainable for some and only partially attainable for others. Admittedly, too, marriage as an institution in present-day America often limps along and falls short of the Christian ideal. But it does not limp and fall short any more frequently than other presumably Christian institutions. Its failures are no argument against it. They are only indications of its inherent potentialities.

IV THE CHRISTIAN WEDDING CEREMONY

From denomination to denomination, from church to church, and even within a given church there is considerable variation in the wording of the wedding ceremony. The ceremony is sometimes modified slightly to fit the needs of a particular couple. In an occasional case the couple write their own ceremony. If they include in it the statements necessary to meet the demands of the church and the law, the ceremony is considered valid. One result of this wide range of variation is that there is no single ceremony that could be quoted in toto here that we could be certain would be or had been used at the wedding of the reader. Therefore, we have chosen to mention phrases that commonly appear in ceremonies either exactly as quoted here or with different phrasing but similar meaning. Several such phrases have already been discussed. The reader may review the ceremony in his own church with this discussion in mind.

CONSENSUS

One of the elements necessary to make the wedding valid in any church is an act and expression of decision and intent on the part of the couple, a mutual agreement to be married. The technical term applied to this is " consensus." It may be expressed as " I do " or as " I will." It is this consensus, not the minister, the state, or the church, which marries the couple.

That is, they marry themselves. But they must do this within the framework required by church and state. If, in a given case, one of the two persons participates in the ceremony through force or duress, or is unable legally to agree to be married (for example, an individual under the legal age for marriage, a feeble-minded individual, or a person already married), or was unaware at the time of the ceremony of the true identity or condition of the other party (for example, in case of fraud or misrepresentation), the marriage is subject to annulment.

When consensus is expressed through the phrase "I will," this denotes, not the future tense of the verb, but rather an act of will, a decision. The question means "Do you will to . . . ?" The answer is, "I will to . . ." If the word "will" were intended to mean the future tense of the verb, the correct form would be "I shall." This is an important consideration, especially when we think in terms of the significance and meaning of the statement, not to the church or the state, but to the individual who makes it. Church and state accept the statement as agreement to be married. The bride and groom ought to interpret it as agreement, plus determination, acceptance, and commitment. When the minister says, "Wilt thou have this Woman to thy wedded wife?" the groom answers, "I will." He is not uttering a mild consent, a simple yes. He is, or certainly should be, saying, "With all the best in my personality, by a carefully considered and profound act of will, with full awareness of what I am doing, I will to have her."

The statements to which each person says "I will" or "I do" are typically the same for both. There is no double standard of responsibility or intent. Jesus, too, drew no lines of distinction or discrimination between the sexes. To him they both were persons, each having the same inherent core of humanity. Few wedding ceremonies nowadays include a promise to obey on the part of the bride. Many do, however, not necessarily require that the bride be "given away," but they take it for granted and make allowance for it.

WEDDING CUSTOMS

The wedding as a whole, with its attendant beliefs and practices, as distinguished from the words of the ceremony itself, is a curious complex of religious, legal, personal, societal, traditional, and even superstitious elements. The very term "wedding" is a carry-over from ancient times. Originally, the wed in marriages was the goods or money that the prospective groom turned over to the father of the prospective bride in order to secure her purchase. The throwing of rice is thought by some originally to have been an offering to the spirits either to appease the evil ones or to further the fertility of the newly married couple. Old shoes are sometimes thrown after the couple or are tied to the vehicle in which they depart following the ceremony. This custom is thought to be a carry-over of the early practice of sealing a bargain or transferring authority or property by means of a shoe. One interesting instance of this is to be found in the story of Ruth and Boaz (Ruth 3:1 to 4:13). The "something old, something new, something borrowed, and something blue" worn by the bride may be attributed in part to the practice of the ancient Jews, who were bidden to wear blue on the borders of their garments in order to signify purity, loyalty, and fidelity. Blue being the color of the "heavens," it was to remind the wearer to remember the commandments of God (Num. 15:38-39). Blue is still used to describe loyalty, fidelity, and quality. For example, we say, "He's true blue." "He's a blue blood." A blue ribbon is used to signify the highest award in a contest. The bridal veil may originally have been a means of distinguishing between a married and an unmarried woman, or a means of disguising the bride to protect her from the evil spirits. Or it may be a reflection of the ancient Jewish custom of holding a canopy over the couple during the wedding ceremony. Such a canopy is still used in the present-day orthodox Jewish ceremony. The use of a ring to symbolize a token or pledge, or as a sign of authority, dates from very early times. For example, Pharaoh transferred a ring from his hand to Joseph's after the latter had interpreted the ruler's dream. (Gen. 41:42.) Among the early Anglo-Saxons the wed mentioned above included a ring, to be worn on the bride's right hand until the time of the wedding and then to be transferred to her left hand. A ring, being a circle and, therefore, having no end, is a readily understood symbol of the permanent nature of marriage. Wedding rings were used by Christians at least as early as the ninth century.

The wedding attendants, with the possible exception of the best man, now have principally a decorative function. They may be derived from the ten witnesses, usually members of the bride's family, required in ancient Rome, or from the parties of friends and relatives of the bride and groom, the former to help protect, the latter to help procure the woman, when marriage was by capture. The practice of the bride's throwing her bouquet may be a modification of the fourteenth-century French custom of the guests' trying to procure one of the garters of the bride for " good luck." During the fifteenth century this gave way to the bride's throwing one of her stockings, which was, no doubt, more convenient for her, but still not so convenient as her throwing her bouquet.

Some folks fear that the groom's seeing the bride before the ceremony on the wedding day will bring " bad luck." Did this fear arise when the bride's parents sought to prevent elopement so that they would not be cheated out of the bride price? Or was its origin the belief that the groom could direct evil spirits or the " evil eye " to the ever-vulnerable bride? Wedding bells and noisemakers associated with the wedding may have their origin in devices to frighten off evil spirits. The groom's carrying the bride over the threshold of their new home may have originated in ancient Rome, where the threshold was considered to be sacred to Vesta, the goddess of virgins. It was thought to be an ill omen if the bride stumbled over the threshold. To prevent such an accident, the groom carried her into the house.

We continue such ancient customs, long since having lost

sight of their origin, just because they are customary or for some vague and ill-defined "good luck" or to avoid "bad luck." But such customs do give us a side light on the antiquity of marriage. They suggest, among other things, that when a couple marry, they establish, of course, a new interpersonal relationship; but they also step into the stream of custom and establish a relationship that society has felt important enough to be meticulously defined and regulated throughout mankind's history and most certainly much of prehistory and among all peoples in the world.

THE CLASPING OF HANDS

During the ceremony the couple clasp their right hands. This adds an element of symbolic personal physical contact. When two individuals bring parts of their bodies together in an acceptable way that has customary meaning, to a degree the barrier between them is broken down and they share each other. To some extent, however slight, a community, a union, a oneness, is set up between them. Shaking hands as a token of friendship, kissing as an expression of affection, are types of physical contact with such symbolic meaning. In some churches there is a "laying on of hands" in confirmation. In the wedding ceremony, a symbol of community, of union, of oneness, is achieved through the clasping of hands.

MARITAL ADJUSTMENT IMPLIED

The wedding proper is typically a relatively brief ceremony. It requires only a few minutes. Yet it marks one of the most profound and significant transitions in human life. In a few words it brings to a sharp focus the essence of marital adjustment distilled, as it were, into a crystal-clear drop of meaning. "Wilt thou have this Woman to thy wedded wife, to live together after God's ordinance in the holy estate of Matrimony? Wilt thou love her, comfort her, honour, and keep her in sick-

ness and in health; and, forsaking all others, keep thee only
unto her, so long as ye both shall live?" And, "I . . . take
thee . . . to my wedded Wife, to have and to hold from this
day forward, for better for worse, for richer for poorer, in sickness and in health, to love and to cherish, till death us do part,
according to God's holy ordinance; and thereto I plight thee
my troth." The bride makes identical promises.

These statements, brief as they are, put marriage "in a
nutshell." They suggest (1) that Christian marriage is basically religious; (2) that marriage is an exclusive relationship;
(3) that each individual accepts the other as that person is;
(4) that, in spite of possible shortcomings, they will love and
respect each other; (5) that problems of adjustment may well
be anticipated; (6) that they will exert continued effort to
make the marriage succeed; (7) that full realization of the
potentialities in marriage comes only through complete commitment for life, the permanent dedication of husband and
wife to it.

The first two items, namely, that marriage is basically religious and is exclusive, have already been discussed. The third,
acceptance, is a *sine qua non* of successful marriage, the "without which, nothing" upon which marriage rests. It is to be
noted that the statement of acceptance is unqualified. It is a
simple "I take thee." No conditional phrase such as "during
good behavior" or "pending your reform" or "granting that
I remain pleased with my choice" is appended. The acceptance
implied is uncluttered and complete. "A friend," someone has
said, "is one who knows all about you and loves you." How
much more significant this becomes with husband and wife!
To accept a person as that person really is, not as one imagines
him to be or hopes he may become, is truly Christian. It also
suggests one difference between infatuation and love, between
romanticizing and reality. In these days of a high and widely
publicized divorce rate, we sometimes lose sight of the fact
that millions of American couples have somehow found a way
to accept each other as they really are and on this basis to

work out marriages that may not be perfect but, nonetheless, contribute to the persons in them values for which there is nothing they would take in exchange. One of the sources of marital disappointment and disillusionment commonly seen by counselors is found in those cases in which a couple marry on too incomplete acquaintance, only to learn after the wedding what they should have learned about each other before, and then find themselves unable to accept each other as they really are. This sort of thing the counselor sees so often that one is tempted to paraphrase a common colloquialism and tell the unmarried who are contemplating a choice of marriage partner, "Take him, or leave him; but don't take him conditionally."

"I take thee" also implies the full acceptance of the other person as a member of the opposite sex with all that this involves in marriage. An individual cannot fully accept another person as a member of the opposite sex unless he first wholeheartedly accepts his own sexual classification. It is at these points that some individuals to some degree limit the fullness of the acceptance. Some act as if they regret that the spouse is of the other sex and as if they would prefer the spouse to be neuter, in which case the sexual aspect of marriage would present no problem. Others make little effort to understand the differences in attitude, feeling, thinking, behavior between male and female, and are correspondingly confused, baffled, startled, or disappointed when the spouse acts appropriately to his or her sexual classification. In any such behavior, there is an implied assumption that there is something regrettable about sexuality. But, as we indicated earlier, there is nothing like this to be found in Jesus' point of view.

The other side of this picture is that, while one accepts the other party, one is at the same time accepted by that other party. This should give one pause for thought. What greater privilege than to be loved and accepted by another person! What greater responsibility than to receive that love and in the receiving know that another person's happiness has been put into one's own hands, that what one does or thinks or feels can go far toward making or breaking the life of that other one! Through love unearned but freely given and freely received can be found a redemptive experience — in marriage within human limitations, unlimited through God and Jesus Christ. It is no wonder that the ceremony says, " is not by any to be entered into unadvisedly or lightly; but reverently, discreetly, advisedly, soberly, and in the fear of God."

Ego Surrender

The fourth, fifth, and sixth items suggest a realistic awareness that within all marriages there are some problems, some sources of conflict. Marriage can be no more nearly perfect than life and the persons in marriage are perfect. But the soundest approach to imperfection is not evasion or escape, but rather continued striving for perfection. This suggests the seventh item, namely, lifelong commitment. What does this mean in practice? It means dedication. It means perspective. It means ego surrender.

In marriage, lifelong commitment may be thought of in terms of self-surrender. The marriage is more important than either person in it. Furthermore, each person considers the other person as of greater worth than himself. Therefore, he gives up self for this greater-than-self. As the old, isolated, separate self " dies " on the cross of ego surrender, a new self emerges, a self no longer separate and isolated but now an integral part of the new entity — " they become one flesh." This is one of the highest forms of " self-preservation."

A New State of Being

Toward the end of the ceremony, the clergyman says, " I pronounce that they are Man and Wife." When he says this, he is not marrying the couple. He is announcing the fact that they are married and that their marriage falls within the ap-

proved framework and has met the requirements of church
and state. Before he makes this statement, the clergyman sum-
marizes what has happened with such phrases as "have con-
sented together in holy wedlock," "have witnessed the same
before God and this company," "have given and pledged their
troth," "have declared the same by giving and receiving a
Ring and by joining hands." The word "pronounce," in this
connection, means "declare," not "make." It signifies the
recognition of a state of being, as when a physician says, "I
pronounce you well." What is the state of being that is recognized in the wedding?

Once some Pharisees asked Jesus a question concerning
divorce. In answer to the question he said, "But from the beginning of creation, 'God made them male and female.' 'For
this reason a man shall leave his father and mother and be
joined to his wife, and the two shall become one.' So they are
no longer two but one" (Mark 10:6-8). This statement was
not original with Jesus. It was a quotation of Gen. 2:24, which,
as we have indicated, was part of Jesus' "Bible." In this statement Jesus did several things. First, he placed marriage very
high in his scale of values, since he obviously quoted the verse
with approval. Among the Jews in Jesus' day the family was
strongly patriarchal. The husband-father was recognized as the
head of the house. If there were several related families associated, the eldest male had special status. There was not the
emphasis upon youth that is so commonly taken for granted
in this country today. One of the Ten Commandments is
"Honor thy father and thy mother." One of the great con-
tributions of Jewish religious genius was the concept that God
is like a father; and this concept runs through both the Old
and New Testaments. So when Jesus affirmed that the husband-
wife relationship was to take precedence over even that of
child to father and mother, he was placing the relationship
very high in his scale of values.

Secondly, Jesus put his stamp of approval on the physical,
the sexual, union of husband and wife. It seems strange indeed

that what Jesus approved so explicitly, some persons consider to be unclean and regrettable; that what he put so high in his scale of values, some persons consider unworthy of intelligent attention in helping young people to prepare for marriage.

Thirdly, there is an implication of societal oneness. Society tends, in some ways, to think of a married pair, not as separate and isolated individuals, but as " two sides of the same coin." Even the law takes this into account, since a husband or wife cannot be forced to testify in court one against the other. It would be too much like being forced to testify against oneself, something expressly prohibited in our Constitution.

Fourthly, Jesus suggested a spiritual unity. " Spiritual " means, not something connected with spirits, but rather, something related to man's highest aspirations, his greatest possibilities for fulfillment, the central meaning and purpose of his life, the way in which he relates himself to God, his experience of God. In this sense, a husband and wife can form a spiritual entity. When complementary natures are combined in common purpose, a new entity is created. Two men or two women can form a workable partnership, but they do not have the capacity to form a union such as that between a man and a woman. In such a union each becomes the answer to the other's need and thus in turn finds in the other the answer to his own needs. Each merges his individual life into the common life, so that the individual life becomes no longer distinguishable as a thing apart. Each yields self to the greater-than-self, as mentioned earlier. Within the new entity each lives more fully than he could live alone, because he shares the life of the other. The *each* and the *both* become inseparable.

Such an entity is in part beyond description, as are many other facets of life, since vocabulary and communication are so limited. In an attempt to describe it, the wedding ceremony compares it to the " mystical union that is betwixt Christ and his church." The Christian church is sometimes referred to as the " body of Christ." By " church " is meant, not a particular denomination or congregation, but the " company of believers."

We can be sure that the phrase "body of Christ" does not mean that the church is the biological body of Jesus. The use of "body" here refers to an entity, a unity, a oneness. We speak of a legislative body, a body of evidence. "Corpus delicti," which is often assumed to be the body of a murder victim, is actually the body of facts proving that a crime has been committed. In each of these instances, "body" refers to some type of entity, some arrangement by which diverse parts, when considered together, constitute a unity. So it is with Christ and the church. Jesus, the man, existed first as a carpenter and then as a preacher-teacher in Palestine. Jesus, the Christ, exists only in relation to the church. Conversely, a group of people attending a meeting in a certain building is only a group of people, each a separate person and only temporarily together. But that same group of people, when they constitute the Christian church, cannot exist as such without Christ. In a sense, then, Christ and the church are one. True, they may be discussed separately. But, separately neither has meaning. Exactly how this happens to be is not fully explainable; it is partly a matter of faith. It is a "mystical union." Hence, the wedding ceremony is indicating something profoundly meaningful when it suggests that the relation between a man and a woman in marriage is like that between Christ and the church. It is this state of being which the clergyman recognizes toward the end of the ceremony.

Is Marriage a Sacrament?

The wedding ceremony suggests two more questions relative to the nature of marriage: Is marriage a sacrament? and Is marriage indissoluble? The latter question we shall discuss in a later chapter. To the former we shall now direct our attention.

Phrases such as "holy matrimony," "instituted of God," "signifying unto us the mystical union that is betwixt Christ and his church," "holy estate," "God's holy ordinance," "holy wedlock," raise the question, Is marriage a sacrament? A sacrament is defined as "an external, visible sign of internal, invisible (or spiritual) grace." In practice this means that an observable procedure is interpreted as an indication that an individual who participates in that procedure has a spiritual experience. This spiritual experience is not forced upon him merely by his going through the procedure. Nor does he have to go through the procedure to have a spiritual experience. But he does have to go through the procedure to have a specific spiritual experience. Two commonly accepted sacraments in Protestant churches are Baptism and Communion (the Lord's Supper, the Eucharist). Whether Baptism should occur by immersion or by sprinkling, whether an individual should partake of the bread and wine at a Communion rail or in his pew, whether he takes a sip of wine or takes the wine by intinction, are matters of disagreement among the churches. But the important consideration is the essential meaning imputed to the particular ceremony involved.

A sacrament has two " sides," so to speak, a man-side and a God-side. To " go through " Baptism or Communion assuming only a man-side would make such a ceremony a mere ritual. It would be in some ways like a pledge of allegiance to the flag. Such a pledge may be a very significant indication of an individual's attitude toward the flag and toward his country. It may be an expression of respect and patriotism. But whatever happens to the individual is self-generated. There is no assumption that the flag or his country does anything to him when he pledges allegiance. In a sacrament, on the other hand, there is a conviction that man does something and God does something. Through the sacrament man and God meet. To some readers this may appear to be anthropomorphic; it may seem to make God like a human being. But the only way man's relationship to God and God's relationship to man can be described is in terms of human life, for man has no other terms at his disposal. By the same token, the only way man can manifest this two-way relationship is through activities of which man is capable. Jesus recognized this human limitation when he said, "Whoever receives one such child in my name receives me; and whoever receives me, receives not me but him who sent me" (Mark 9:37). In instituting the Lord's Supper, Jesus took everyday materials at hand and utilized one of man's most necessary and most frequently repeated activities, namely, eating and drinking, to establish a memorial to himself and a means by which, through proper interpretation under particular circumstances, man may approach God. Here again we are confronted with a point of faith. Either there is a God or there is no God. If there is a God, either he is accessible to man or he is not accessible to man. If he is accessible, there must be some means by which this is accomplished. Christianity maintains that the means are worship, prayer, service to one's fellow men, and the sacraments.

The Protestant churches are disinclined to consider marriage a true sacrament. But certainly marriage has within it sacramental elements and opportunities. Conceivably, an individual might participate in Baptism or Communion with such participation being merely ritualistic and with the sacramental element bypassed. The internal, spiritual experience is, as mentioned above, not forced upon the individual by the external, visible act. The outward act only gives him the opportunity for the spiritual experience. Whether or not he has it depends in part on what he himself brings to the act. If marriage is interpreted in terms such as this, it is clear that in it may be found opportunities for a sacramental experience.

Most of man's experience has two aspects: the outward observable aspect, that is, how man is observed to react and what he reacts to; and the inward, nonobservable aspect, that is, that part of his total experience which is neither observable nor communicable. For example, an individual sees an exceptionally beautiful sunset. He is observed to react in a given way. He is heard to mention it. But there are three, not only two, elements in this situation. There is the sunset. There is the individual's observable reaction. In addition there is his "inner " response, something that he cannot verbalize, that he cannot communicate, that cannot be observed in any way, and that may affect his future reactions to other people and even his interpretation of and relation to God without its ever being identified as the cause of such reactions or interpretations. In a similar manner an individual may have such an " inner " response to his marriage. This response may color his attitude toward, interpretation of, and relationship to God. If he recognizes such a possibility in marriage, he seeks means of expressing it. Such means he may find in his relationship to his spouse. Conversely, if he has a vital faith in the existence, love, and accessibility of God, and if he himself loves God, then he may seek ways of expressing this faith. The only means he can ever discover must of necessity be found within the circumstances and limitations of human life. Man must find the medium for expressing his love for God in the opportunities that are at hand. Where can such opportunity better be found than in the relationship between husband and wife, which is not only always close at hand but is imbued with special significance?

Redemption is the process by which man is brought back to God. It is the process by which man's separation from God is, through Christ, converted into man's union with God. This, also, is a two-sided situation. There can be no redemption unless God and man both desire it. Christianity affirms that God's love for man is infinite and ever-present and that, therefore, God always seeks man's redemption. Then redemption is available to man at any time that he himself is willing to accept God's love. As already suggested, there is in the giving and accepting of love in marriage the human counterpart of this redemptive process. Love in marriage is itself redemptive. But it is also a channel through which a married pair may utilize something within their experience and therefore at their command, to symbolize the greater redemption. Just as the individual is born separated from God and must return to God through his own choice, so the sexes are born separate, in a state of aloneness, and must be brought together into " one flesh " through the redemptive experience of love, which, too, rests upon their own choice. Redemption is what happens to man's being when he is confronted with, accepts, and in return gives love. This occurs in finite form in marriage. It occurs in infinite form in man's relation to God.

V JESUS' TEACHINGS

THE GOSPELS

The Gospels were not written until decades after Jesus' death. They were written after Paul's Epistles were written. Whereas they appear in the New Testament in this order: Matthew, Mark, Luke, John, they were probably written in this order: Mark, Luke or Matthew, John. This fact is important in interpreting them. Each Gospel writer used the sources of information at his command. In some cases two writers used the same source. It is probable, too, that a later writer such as Matthew used an earlier Gospel such as Mark's as a source. Each writer wrote with a different specific purpose and a different audience in mind. For this reason, we find different emphases, the inclusion of things here and the omission of them there. Also, because of this difference in purpose and audience and the difference in time of writing, we need not be surprised at minor discrepancies. Each Gospel is a summary; and at times different elements of Jesus' life and teachings are combined in different ways. The similarities are more significant than the dissimilarities. The similarities seem all the more significant when we realize that Jesus himself left no written records of his teachings.

THE BEGINNING OF THE CHURCH

One of the most prominent characteristics of the people with whom Jesus came in contact, including people in general and his closest followers, was their persistent failure to comprehend what he was talking about. Over and over again through all four Gospels there are references to such failure in the questions the disciples asked, in the arguments in which they engaged, in the things that they did or failed to do, in their expressions of disillusionment and fear. They became so entangled in a web of self-concern, ignorance of their own Scriptures, emphasis upon the law, anxiety about the future and their role in it, diversion by inconsequential detail, that they missed the central meaning of Jesus' life and teachings. It is amazing that some of them remembered as much as they did.

Up to the very day of the crucifixion this condition of his followers persisted. Immediately after the crucifixion they were more than ever disillusioned and afraid. Their anticipated world had collapsed on the cross. They had pinned their hopes on a man who called himself the Son of God and he had been executed as a common criminal. But somewhere amid all that confusion, fear, and disillusionment, a spark had been ignited. There had been moments when a few had looked at him and seen God. There is far from complete agreement in Christendom as to the exact nature of the events that followed immediately upon Jesus' death. An analysis of precisely what happened is not the province of this book. But of one thing we can be sure. Within a brief time after the crucifixion, something had happened that transformed a frightened little band of believers into a force that is still reverberating throughout the world. Thus a process, an event, an experience, not the details of a written account, is the basic *fact* of Christianity. Since the church was organized and was already an active leaven in human life before the Gospels were written, its continuance can hardly depend upon the exact phrasing of those records.

JESUS' AUDIENCES

No one like Jesus could have avoided acquiring enemies. Through each Gospel runs a thread of increasing hostility and opposition. Again and again there were threats, attempts to trick him in such a way that he would find himself in trouble with the authorities of church or state, plots against him, even the eventual corruption of one of the apostles.

One result of all this was that Jesus did and said different things for different reasons. We cannot assume that everything is to be considered as being in the same category. Some things he did because people in his day naturally did them. For example, he ate with friends. He was criticized for this and the fact that he continued doing it showed something about him; but it is not in the same category as the Lord's Supper.

Some things he said occurred in relation to his central objective. For example, the Beatitudes give the impression of a carefully organized series of principles as in a sermon, and of such nature that they might be included in the basic foundation of Christian living. On the other hand, there were acts of kindness done to meet individuals' personal needs, and statements made to individuals that had meaning in the light of their particular needs but were not necessarily intended as a basis for generalization. For example, when a certain very rich young ruler asked Jesus what he might do to "inherit eternal life," Jesus told him to sell all his possessions and distribute the proceeds to the poor (Luke 18:18-25). Was this intended as a recommendation of general practice or as a direct suggestion to meet the needs of a young man whose dependence upon wealth and the keeping of the details of the law were a barrier to his participation in the Kingdom of God? If literally everyone who had any possessions were to sell them and give the proceeds to the poor, it would only transfer the burden of possessions to the previously poor, who would then be the ones who were rich. A vicious circle would be set up. Obviously, Jesus did not have this in mind. He was saying something about possessions that had universal significance but with a particular application to the young man. We do not mean to imply that persons favored with wealth have no obligations to the less fortunate. But a literal interpretation of Jesus' recommendation to the young ruler logically eventuates in such things as vows of poverty, which, again, may be meaningful to the persons making the vows, but are not feasible in present-day industrial society unless someone other than the avower holds possessions.

Sometimes Jesus spoke to a friendly audience of persons eager to learn. Some were more perceptive than others. Some were outright obtuse. At other times he spoke to a hostile audience, the members of which pretended to be eager to learn but actually had no interest in learning. They asked questions, not for information, but to trick him. Can we safely assume that every statement Jesus made may be interpreted without regard to the friendliness or hostility of the audience? We must keep this in mind in the next chapter, because most of the statements Jesus made concerning marriage and divorce were made to a hostile audience.

NATURE OF JESUS' TEACHINGS

In his public teaching and preaching, Jesus must have said many things that are not recorded in the Gospels. As suggested earlier, what is recorded is a summary of "high spots" and things that for one reason or another struck an individual and remained in his memory. Many steps, some known and some not, occurred between Jesus' original verbal statements and our present-day revised version of the New Testament. Along the way there were additions and subtractions, errors in recording and translation, items included to clarify something for a particular type of reader, new interpretations and emphases. Because the Gospels were written for readers who were already familiar with many details of background and practice, these details were omitted. This omission is confusing and misleading to readers today. Therefore, it becomes a mistake to extract a particular statement or incident from its historical and cultural background and from the totality of Jesus' teaching and to interpret it as if it were unrelated to anything else. Everything that Jesus said ought to be interpreted against the background of his over-all thought and objective. If this is not done, we fall into the same error as the Jews of Jesus' day, who spun out interpretations of the law until they became so fine that they became meaningless trivialities.

Jesus was not a lawgiver. He was a propounder of principle, an expounder of fundamental truth. Because of this, his teachings are characterized by a certain simplicity as compared to the complexities involved in formulating law. His major emphasis was placed on the human spirit, that is, the motives and attitudes underlying human action. He was more interested in the meaning of an act than in the act per se. He repeatedly penetrated behind a given statement, act, law, or practice to its significance for human personality. In neither his teaching nor his acts is human personality ever subordinated to legalism. For example, "The sabbath was made for man, and not man for the sabbath." (Mark 2:27.) He taught that all the important elements of the law could be expressed in two simply stated principles: "You shall love the Lord your God with all your heart, and with all your soul, and with all your mind, and with all your strength. . . . You shall love your neighbor as yourself" (Mark 12:30-31).

VALIDITY OF JESUS' TEACHINGS

There is a special validity to Jesus' teachings. On the one hand, this grows out of his unique relationship to God. On the other, it grows out of his insight into the true nature of man. He described man as man is. In so doing, he made an underlying assumption, recognized an underlying truth. Man is born with great capacity to learn. Much that he becomes is the result of the interaction between his inborn traits or capacity and his experience within his environment. He is subject to numerous conditioning processes. To a considerable degree, on the one hand, his behavior is determined by forces beyond his control. His personality is in part culturally determined. On the other hand, he has considerable free will and freedom of choice. Nevertheless, man is also the product of a long creative evolutionary process. His particular structure and capacity to function contribute a certain constant core to man's nature. He is not infinitely variable. There are some things true about him because he is man. This fact establishes a special relativity regardless of his culture, his time of appearance in history, his experience, his particular personality.

When, for example, Jesus said, "Whoever would save his life will lose it; and whoever loses his life for my sake and the gospel's will save it" (Mark 8:35), he was not merely formulating an interesting philosophical concept; he was describing the nature of man. He was doing a similar thing when he said, "It is more blessed to give than to receive" (Acts 20:35). In effect, this is the equivalent of saying that no matter where man is found, at any time in any culture, he is so constituted that his deepest satisfactions and highest personality development in the "long run" come through giving rather than through getting, through ego surrender rather than ego aggrandizement. That is the way man is. Such penetrating to the heart of man's basic nature is characteristic of Jesus' teaching.

VI JESUS AND DIVORCE

One of the most controversial statements in the New Testament is Jesus' statement concerning divorce. (Mark 10:2-12; Matt. 19:3-9.) Before we attempt an interpretation, let us try to reconstruct the occasion on which the statement was made. This is difficult because the Gospels of Mark and Matthew do not agree, and because, therefore, scholars disagree as to what Jesus actually or probably said. We must keep in mind that the book of Mark was written earlier than that of Matthew, that it is highly likely that Matthew and perhaps both used the so-called Q source, and that it is probable that Matthew also used Mark's book as a source.

Marriage and Divorce in Jesus' Day

In Jesus' day marriages were arranged by parents or through an intermediary. Young people had some choice in the matter but not the freedom of choice that we take for granted in this country today. Romantic courtship as we know it was not practiced. Before the wedding there was an exchange of goods or services. This, plus the then current attitude toward women, gave the husband a property right in the wife. She was, however, not a chattel so that he could resell her. Conjugal love often developed in marriage; but romantic love was not considered the basis for marriage. Betrothal was not the same as present-day engagement. A betrothed couple were only a shade different from a married couple. For a betrothal to be dissolved required a bill of divorce just as the dissolution of a marriage did. A betrothed woman whose fiancé died was considered a widow. Betrothal became marriage when the bridegroom took the bride to his home and the consummation of the marriage took place. This explains Matthew 1:18, which otherwise is confusing to readers today: " Now the birth of Jesus Christ took place in this way. When his mother Mary had been betrothed to Joseph, before they came together she was found to be with child of the Holy Spirit; and her husband Joseph, being a just man and unwilling to put her to shame, resolved to divorce her quietly." Although the couple were only betrothed, Joseph was referred to as Mary's husband.

Divorce, as suggested above, occurred through a bill of divorce, according to the law of Moses: "When a man takes a wife and marries her, if then she finds no favor in his eyes because he has found some indecency in her, and he writes her a bill of divorce and puts it in her hand and sends her out of his house, and she departs out of his house, and if she goes and becomes another man's wife . . ." (Deut. 24:1-2). Remarriage was clearly acceptable. In fact, there was little else for a divorced woman to do. While the law gave the husband the privilege of divorcing the wife merely by giving her a written statement to the effect that the divorce had occurred, no similar privilege was accorded the wife. In rare cases she could require him to divorce her. It was only after the Hebrews came into contact with other cultures, such as that of Rome, that women acquired a right of divorce comparable to that of men.

Adultery was considered to be an offense against the husband. It could be committed only by or with the married. Since the husband had complete and exclusive control of the wife's sexuality, while she had no corresponding control of his, only a wife could commit adultery. The husband, or for that matter any man married or unmarried, was guilty of an offense if his sexual partner were a married woman. But a married man could not commit adultery with an unmarried woman. There was, therefore, a double standard, in important respects different from that which we have today, but nonetheless present and commonly understood.

As indicated above, according to the Mosaic law a man could divorce his wife "if . . . she finds no favor in his eyes because he has found some indecency in her." This is a broad and somewhat ambiguous statement. It is the sort of statement that is ready prey for shifting interpretations as time goes on and as conditions change. At best, it left much to the judgment and discretion of the husband. The result was that as time went on divorce became common in Israel. It sometimes occurred for trivial reasons. It was even possible for a man to divorce his wife without explaining the reason to her. This condition led to disputes and debates as to the meaning of the law. One is reminded of our present-day situation relative to the meaning of "cruelty" as a ground for divorce. Some insist that "cruelty" should be restricted to extreme cruelty, especially physical brutality. Others allow for a great variety of definitions. In some courts the most trivial offenses are adjudged to be cruelty of sufficient seriousness as to permit the granting of divorce. One has only to read the newspaper to see reports of divorce cases in which decrees were granted on the alleged grounds of behavior that could only within the most lax definition be considered cruel.

In like manner there were debates among the rabbis as to what was meant in the law by "if . . . she finds no favor in his eyes because he has found some indecency in her." What was such an "indecency"? One school of rabbis, that led by Shammai, was very strict in its interpretation. Rabbis in this group insisted that the law applied only to something extreme such as adultery. To the rabbis in the Shammai school of thought, divorce was an abomination, a necessary evil, a regrettable last resort. The rabbis in the Hillel school of thought, on the other hand, interpreted the law freely and with great leniency. They approved divorce for such relatively trivial offenses as a wife's burning or oversalting her husband's food or a husband's finding another woman who appealed to him more than his wife. Because of such disagreement there emerged a multiplicity of accepted grounds for divorce. This fact, coupled with the fact that almost the entire right of divorce rested with the husband, must have made the marital situation very insecure and unpalatable for many a wife in Jesus' day.

JESUS' STATEMENTS REGARDING DIVORCE

As indicated earlier, the interpretation of any statement by Jesus should be made in the light of his total teaching, against the background of the times in which he lived, and with relation to the audience to which it was addressed. His statement regarding divorce was made, in part at least, to a hostile male audience, a group of Pharisees who wanted, not information, not a statement of principle, but a way to trap him. Shall we assume that that statement represents his total attitude toward the subject, that it was all that he had to say, and would not have been modified or elaborated upon in any way had the audience and circumstances been different?

" And Pharisees came up and in order to test him asked, ' Is it lawful for a man to divorce his wife? ' He answered them, ' What did Moses command you? ' They said, ' Moses allowed a man to write a certificate of divorce, and to put her away.' But Jesus said to them, ' For your hardness of heart he wrote you this commandment. But from the beginning of creation, " God made them male and female." " For this reason a man shall leave his father and mother and be joined to his wife, and the two shall become one." So they are no longer two but one. What therefore God has joined together, let not man put asunder.'

" And in the house the disciples asked him again about this matter. And he said to them, ' Whoever divorces his wife and marries another, commits adultery against her; and if she divorces her husband and marries another, she commits adultery.' " (Mark 10:2-12.)

Matthew reports Jesus' entire statement as having been made to the Pharisees. After " divorce one's wife " Matthew adds " for any cause." Did this refer to the multiplicity of grounds for divorce accepted by the Hillel school or did it suggest the rare exception? After the phrase "Whoever divorces his wife," Matthew adds "except for unchastity." (Matt. 19:3-9.) In another place, in a collection of Jesus' teachings, Matthew shifts the meaning somewhat: "It was also said, 'Whoever divorces his wife, let him give her a certificate of divorce. But I say to you that every one who divorces his wife, except on the ground of unchastity, makes her an adulteress; and whoever marries a divorced woman commits adultery" (Matt. 5:31-32). This raises important questions. To whom did Jesus really make the statement about adultery? Was the phrase "except for unchastity" originally used by Jesus and then omitted by Mark? Or was it not part of Jesus' original statement and then later added by Matthew? Many scholars lean toward the latter view. But because of this discrepancy between the two books, it is difficult to know just what Jesus did say about divorce.

The Pharisees were crafty. The question they asked could be answered in no way that would not put Jesus into apparent disagreement with either the Shammai or the Hillel school of thought. The question also made Jesus take a stand on the Mosaic law. Furthermore, at the time, Jesus was traveling through the territory of Herod, who had divorced his wife to marry Herodias.

Jesus was not a lawgiver. Therefore, we cannot assume that in his statement about divorce he was formulating a new law. Perhaps we should not subject it to detailed dissection. When, however, we do look at the recorded statements word by word, what do we find? Assuming that Mark's account is more nearly accurate than Matthew's, we find that Jesus did not explicitly prohibit divorce. There is no place where he says there should be no divorce. He does imply it in the statement regarding adultery, and he does express himself as disapproving remarriage of the divorced. Assuming that Matthew's account is more nearly accurate than Mark's, Jesus did define one possible acceptable ground for divorce, namely, unchastity.

This would make his statement mean that if a marriage had already been destroyed by unfaithfulness, it could not be further destroyed by divorce.

In the statement "What therefore God has joined together, let not man put asunder" (Mark 10:9), Jesus could not have been referring to every individual marriage. Can it be assumed that every marriage, no matter under what circumstances it occurs, no matter what the age, maturity, condition of the couple at the time of the wedding, represents two persons joined by God? If we assume this, we are assuming that God is party to many a tragic mistake or else that the words a couple utter during the wedding ceremony contain a certain magic that forces God's approval of the marriage. It is sounder to assume that, since the Pharisees had asked about the institution of marriage rather than a particular marriage, Jesus answered in the same vein. The institution of marriage was being undermined by men who were abusing the right of divorce and thus violating the relationship of husband and wife that had been ordained by God. It was being profaned by men who took for granted a man's right to "put away" his wife as if a woman were a thing to be retained or discarded at a man's caprice, by men who sometimes divorced their wives to marry more attractive women.

The various statements concerning divorce are both conflicting and ambiguous. "Whoever divorces his wife and marries another, commits adultery against her." (Mark 10:11.) Against whom is the adultery: the former wife or the new one? "If she divorces her husband and marries another, she commits adultery." (Mark 10:12.) Technically the wife could not divorce the husband. "Every one who divorces his wife and marries another commits adultery, and he who marries a woman divorced from her husband commits adultery." (Luke 16:18.) "Every one who divorces his wife, except on the ground of unchastity, makes her an adulteress; and whoever marries a divorced woman commits adultery." (Matt. 5:32.) Each of these statements, except part of the last one, "makes her an adulteress," mentions remarriage. If the divorced persons do not remarry, do they then commit adultery? How could they? In the statement "makes her an adulteress" there may either be an implied remarriage because there was little else for the woman to do, or else we must assume the impossible implication that a woman commits adultery merely by becoming divorced. In any case, if, as some insist, Jesus implied that there was no possible breaking of the marriage bond, would he not have had to say that whoever divorces his wife and marries another or whoever marries a divorced woman commits, not adultery, but bigamy? If the couple are still married, what can "marries another" or "marries a divorced woman" possibly mean? Jesus himself was implying that divorce severed the marriage bond. If we assume that Jesus was implying that the couple were still united by an unbreakable spiritual bond even though they had been divorced within the law and were, therefore, legally able to remarry, we are assuming that a spiritual bond is sustained by some sort of pressure, or force, or inflexible obligation to a vow. A spiritual bond, like love, cannot continue to exist except through free and voluntary commitment.

We must remember that Jesus was asked a test question by a group of hostile males who believed that a man could not commit adultery. In the statements Jesus made, he made it clear that a man could be fully as guilty of adultery as a woman could be. Adultery did not depend upon one's sex. It depended upon what one did, regardless of sex. This is consistent with other of Jesus' teachings, attitudes, and behavior relative to the sexes.

In the last analysis, it appears that we are forced to an admission that is in accord with the known facts but is not acceptable to persons who think in terms of what might be referred to as compulsive absolutes. Such folks are uncomfortable when historical evidence or lack of it leaves some question unanswered or some problem "open ended." They want to remove every inconsistency, to convert every principle into an inflexible rule, to define every detail of human behavior in such a way that freedom of judgment is reduced to obedience. The admission to which we are forced is this: we do not know precisely what Jesus said about divorce, and furthermore, we do not know exactly how to interpret the recorded fragments of what he said. This leaves us with only one acceptable alternative, namely, to interpret his recorded statements against the background of his total personality and teachings.

When we do this, it becomes clear that in his discussion with the Pharisees, Jesus did with divorce as he had done with many another topic: he penetrated the externals and went to the core of the problem. He penetrated practice and put his finger on principle. He spoke in terms of the perfect ideal, all the while aware that human beings had the capacity to strive for it but not the capacity to achieve it. In fact, he implied that last point when he said to the disciples after the discussion with the Pharisees, " Not all men can receive this precept, but only those to whom it is given " (Matt. 19:11).

To Jesus the essential nature of marriage was spiritual. Husband and wife formed complementary parts of a new entity; they became one, " one flesh." This union is a matter of choice; they leave their parents and are joined to each other, as the book of Genesis suggests. They are not bound together by external pressure or by force, though they may be held together by law.

As indicated earlier, Jesus never subordinated human welfare or human personality to legalism. He taught that the motive underlying an act was more important, in some ways, than the act itself; that in the last analysis it was his attitudes and not his overt behavior by which an individual was to be judged. He taught in terms of principles, not rules. Time and again he made it clear that what a person did, even though it might appear on the surface to be very good, was of no avail unless the individual was right with God and his fellow men. This applied even to making gifts to the church. (Matt. 5:23-24.) He emphasized the principle of the second chance, the right of an individual to the opportunity to correct a mistake, to start again. He maintained that institutions were made for man, not man for institutions. He insisted that human beings never be forced into empty form when all substance was gone.

Thinking in terms of human welfare rather than law and rule, in terms of function rather than structure, Jesus would not be one to insist that a couple remain in a loveless marriage anchored in hate, distrust, indifference, lack of mutual concern, the cramping of personality, merely in order to protect institutional form. He would recognize that in some cases remaining in such a marriage could be more damaging to personality than would dissolving the legal structure when the spiritual function was already dead. To refuse a couple the opportunity to recognize and correct a mistake and to start again would be like preserving the body after life had been destroyed. If Jesus expounded a new law or formulated a new and inflexible rule regarding divorce, as some persons maintain, then this would constitute a unique exception to all of his teaching. Such an exception cannot be substantiated by what we know of him. Divorce, like surgery, is often a regrettable necessity; and Jesus would share our concern today over the need for it. Too easy, irresponsible, hasty divorce that is detrimental to both the couple and the institution of marriage, Jesus would no doubt regret and disapprove of today just as he did in his discussion with the Pharisees. Here again there can be a central principle, namely, the possibility of divorce when appropriate for the furtherance of human welfare, which is not to be judged only by current practice. Whether or not the phrase " except it be for unchastity " was used by Jesus, we know it was not recorded by Mark. We know also, however, that it was recorded by Matthew. This means that Matthew was inclined to present his readers with a loophole of exception that, in light of the times and the circumstances under which his readers lived, he felt was acceptable. Since Matthew was closer to Jesus than we are and since he therefore knew more about both the recorded and the omitted details of Jesus' life and teaching, his inclination to allow this exception should give us pause for thought. Whatever may be the correct interpretation of Jesus' statements, the fact remains that Protestant churches do accept and permit divorce. They also accept remarriage and in so doing do not adjudge the individuals involved as adulterous.

One prominent characteristic of Jesus' teaching was an emphasis upon the positive. If we permit ourselves to become so diverted by a consideration of the technicalities of the problem of divorce that we forget the central emphasis on the essentially spiritual nature of marriage, we do precisely what Jesus criticized in the Pharisees.

REMARRIAGE AFTER DIVORCE

Some churches, however, fall into a trap relative to the problem of remarriage. They do this in their greater willingness to approve of the remarriage of the "innocent" party, in a case of divorce, than that of the "guilty" party. This black-white distinction between the parties to a divorce is nowadays seen to be untenable. Divorce law, and consequently court interpretations, is based on the principle of contest and injury, that is, adversary litigation. The underlying assumption is that one spouse, who is pure-black guilty, commits an offense that injures the other spouse, who is pure-white innocent. This offense and its resultant injury are defined by the law and constitute grounds for divorce. The result is that many couples "trump up" grounds for divorce and fit their marriage-divorce situations into the framework of the law, even if they have to misrepresent the facts in order to do so.

Present-day understanding of marriage and divorce, however, suggests that the principle of injury and contest does not adequately fit the actual situation. What happens is this: a couple find that they no longer love each other as they originally did, or one no longer loves the other as at first, and they cannot get along together happily. There are a thousand and

one details of incompatibility, numerous focal points of conflict. Then one of two things usually happens. Either the couple
fit their situation into the law, one claiming as a ground for
divorce some offense that the other does not deny, or the incompatibility leads one of them actually to commit some offense, such as adultery or desertion, which can then be used
as a ground for divorce. In very few, if any, divorce cases is
only one spouse at fault. In practically all, if not indeed all,
both persons share the blame for the failure of the marriage.
In any case, they share the blame because, at the time of the
wedding, each took responsibility for the success of the marriage. So the principle of injury and contest, as established in
the law, is no longer in accord with the facts. Therefore, when
a church looks with greater favor on the remarriage of the
" innocent " party than on the remarriage of the " guilty "
party, it is falling into the same trap as the law. To make the
assumption that the distinction between the innocent and the
guilty may be made by ascertaining which was plaintiff and
which defendant in the divorce action is completely unsound.
There is still another weakness in the position of any church
that makes a distinction between the " guilty " and the " innocent " relative to remarriage. How is relative guilt or innocence
to be determined? In many cases the only one of the ex-
spouses who can be asked is the one who wants to remarry
within a given church. Counseling experience suggests that
it is never safe to make an appraisal of one spouse exclusively
on the basis of the unavoidably biased statements of the other,
and it is never safe to make a complete appraisal of a marriage
even on the testimony of both, since neither can state the facts
objectively; each must of necessity give his own interpretation
of the facts.

" Till Death Us Do Part "

Whatever may have been Jesus' attitude toward divorce and
the churches' stand upon it, what shall we make of " so long

as ye both shall live" and "till death us do part" to which the couple express agreement in the wedding ceremony? Before an answer to this question is attempted at all, these phrases must be examined in their relation to the total ceremony. As with Biblical verses, they should not be taken out of context.

In discussing these phrases we shall have to generalize somewhat since they are not necessarily found in exactly the same form in every ceremony. But we shall discuss what is fairly typical.

The first phrase, "so long as ye both shall live," is part of a statement that has, among others, two pertinent characteristics. "Wilt thou have this Woman to thy wedded wife, to live together after God's ordinance in the holy estate of Matrimony? Wilt thou love her, comfort her, honour, and keep her in sickness and in health; and, forsaking all others, keep thee only unto her, so long as ye both shall live?" To this the man answers "I will." A similar statement is made by the woman. The use of "wilt" and "will" here, as we pointed out in an earlier connection, does not indicate the future tense of the verb. If it did, a question would be raised as to when — "When in the future will you have this woman to your wedded wife?" Rather, the use of "wilt" and "will" indicates an act of will, a decision, a commitment. This act of will involves a commitment to live together "after God's ordinance in the holy estate of Matrimony," to love, comfort, honor, and protect someone, to remain true to that person for life. It does not involve merely a promise to remain married for life. If the definition of "wilt" is shifted in the second sentence, the essential meaning of the commitment is changed. Some persons would read the sentence this way: "Will [an act of will] you love her, comfort her, honor, and keep her in sickness and in health; and forsaking all others, will you [this is understood and implies the future tense] keep only unto her, so long as you both shall live?" This is not the intended meaning.

The context of the second phrase is this: "I, ——, take thee, ——, to my wedded wife, to have and to hold from this day forward, for better for worse, for richer for poorer, in sickness and in health, to love and to cherish, till death us do part, according to God's holy ordinance; and thereto I plight thee my troth." There are two elements in this statement. On the one hand, there is the element of accepting the other person for the future and regardless of conditions. An individual could make such a promise and through courage and determination adhere to it. On the other hand, however, there is the matter of loving and cherishing for life "according to God's holy ordinance." In both this statement and the one in the paragraph above, a most important question is raised: Can anyone promise to love another person and live with that person in the "holy estate of Matrimony" for life? He can promise to live with that person in marriage. But he cannot promise to love that person and to make that marriage a spiritual one, a holy estate. No human being has the capacity for such a promise. To such an end he may make a most solemn commitment, but that is not an unalterable promise.

So we may interpret the phrases "so long as ye both shall live" and "till death us do part" as statements of unreserved commitment, of most profound intent. Without such unconditional commitment Christian marriage would be impossible. Marriage only begins, it is not completed, at the time of the wedding. To be oriented toward the proper goal, it must begin with the proper commitment. To assume that these two phrases bind a couple for life, no matter what their relationship may be, is to assume that marriage not only begins but also is completed in the wedding ceremony. It puts the primary emphasis upon structure rather than upon function, upon form rather than upon meaning, upon stability rather than upon spirituality.

There may be some who will say that the above is rationalization and that it seriously weakens the entire concept of Christian marriage. Actually, instead of weakening it, it strengthens that concept. It places the emphasis where it belongs, namely, upon the ultimate ideal. It emphasizes the spiritual aspects of marriage as against the outward form. It emphasizes human personality as against legalism. It incorporates Jesus' principle of the second chance. It implies that a true marriage, and especially a Christian marriage, is not preserved by form or force, by law or doctrine, but only by the capacity of the couple, through love, to establish and sustain a spiritual unity. If in their marital relationship they have ceased to be one, " one flesh," no amount or kind of resistance to divorce can make them one and no approval of divorce can make them less one. If their marriage fails functionally, it cannot be made to succeed merely by preserving it structurally. This does not make marriage tentative, as some folks insist. It does not imply that when they marry, couples " leave the back door open." It merely recognizes human capacities and limitations and the true nature of marriage.

VII JESUS AND PAUL

PAUL AND HIS WRITINGS

Paul, the great missionary who carried the gospel to the Greek and Roman world, was born in the city of Tarsus during the lifetime of Jesus; but the two never met. Paul was a Jew whose father was a Roman citizen. He was educated in the synagogue and became a Pharisee. Even as a young man he was deeply interested in the Mosaic law; and he was more than ordinarily zealous in seeking to make his life righteous according to that law. It was this very zeal which led him to be active in the effort to wipe out the early Christian church, an activity that eventuated in his conversion. This zeal for righteousness remained characteristic of Paul throughout his life, and we see it expressed over and again in his writings.

Paul's writings, in so far as they are preserved in the New Testament, consist of letters. These letters, even though they are put after the Gospels in the New Testament, were written before the Gospels were written; so we must not assume that Paul could refer to the Gospels as we do. What Paul knew about Jesus he derived from other sources. The letters were addressed to individuals and to Greek and Roman churches already established. These churches, like present-day churches, had questions and problems. There were questions of doctrine, of interpretation, of historical fact. There were problems of organization, of working out the relationship between the members of the churches and the communities in which they lived, of maintaining a Christian point of view and faith in the midst of idolatry, immorality, oppression, and persecution.

Paul was deeply concerned about the churches. He visited those which he could when he could. When he could not visit, he sent letters. It is not surprising that much of what he wrote was directed to specific questions and problems in particular congregations. " Now concerning the matters about which you wrote." (I Cor. 7:1.) In interpreting Paul's letters this fact must be kept in mind.

Another thing that must be kept in mind is that Paul anticipated the early return of Jesus the Christ and the end of an era. To this expectation Paul gave considerable prominence, and this relegated many other things to positions of secondary importance. For example, he wrote of the "impending distress " (I Cor. 7:26). He said, " The appointed time has grown very short " (I Cor. 7:29); " the form of this world is passing away " (I Cor. 7:31).

Still another fact that must be kept in mind in interpreting Paul's writings is that he apparently was not married, at least, not at the time he wrote his letters. Whether he had ever been married is uncertain. Jesus never married. But we may safely assume that there were significant differences between the singleness of Jesus and that of Paul. Paul sets up his own status as a model to be copied if possible. " To the unmarried and the widows I say that it is well for them to remain single as I do." (I Cor. 7:8.) Paul's writings, then, should be examined against the backdrop of their textual and circumstantial context.

PAUL'S STAND ON IMMORALITY

The Greek and Roman churches were tiny islands of Christianity surrounded by a sea of paganism. The ones to which Paul wrote were in cities. Life was considered to be very cheap in Greece and Rome. Many a Christian lost his life for no other reason than that he was a Christian. To take a stand on Christian faith often meant taking a stand on life itself.

In these Greek and Roman cities sexual immorality ran rampant. There were even individuals who not only condoned it but advocated it. This led some of the early Christians to misconstrue the doctrine of salvation by grace not by works. They reasoned that since they would be saved by grace, it made no difference what happened to the body. Hence, it was easy to fall into the trap of rationalizing sexual license.

Paul took a clear-cut unyielding position in opposition to sexual license. " It is actually reported that there is immorality among you, and of a kind that is not found even among pagans; for a man is living with his father's wife. . . . Let him who has done this be removed from among you." (I Cor. 5:1-2.) " The body is not made for immorality." (I Cor. 6:13.) " Shun immorality." (I Cor. 6:18.) " For this is the will of God, your sanctification: that you abstain from immorality." (I Thess. 4:3.)

PAUL AND DIVORCE

Paul made brief references to divorce, and his stand on it was negative. (I Cor. 7:10-11.) He did, however, approve of divorce if one spouse was a believer and the other a non-believer and it was the latter who wanted to dissolve the marriage. (I Cor. 7:12-15.) In the later history of the church this came to be known as the " Pauline privilege."

PAUL'S ATTITUDE TOWARD WOMEN

There seems to be no doubt that Paul relegated women to a position of inferiority to men. For example, " I want you to understand that the head of every man is Christ, the head of a woman is her husband, and the head of Christ is God." (I Cor. 11:3.) " The women should keep silence in the churches. For they are not permitted to speak, but should be

subordinate, even as the law says. If there is anything they desire to know, let them ask their husbands at home. For it is
shameful for a woman to speak in church." (I Cor. 14:34-35.)
" Wives, be subject to your husbands, as to the Lord." (Eph.
5:22.) The fact that Paul repeats this statement in his letter to
the Colossians (Col. 3:18) gives it emphasis. " I permit no
woman to teach or to have authority over men; she is to keep
silent." (I Tim. 2:12.)

PAUL'S ATTITUDE TOWARD MARRYING

Paul's statements regarding marriage are mixed and varied.
On the one hand, he seems reluctant, regretful, conceding. We
do not find in him the wholehearted, enthusiastic acceptance
and approval that we find in Jesus. To Paul marriage was a
sort of secondary value, a necessary concession to human biology but something of such nature that to forgo it indicated
strength of character. For example: " It is well for a man not
to touch a woman. But because of the temptation to immorality, each man should have his own wife and each woman her
own husband." (I Cor. 7:1-2.) " I wish that all were as I myself am." (I Cor. 7:7.) " To the unmarried and the widows I
say that it is well for them to remain single as I do. But if
they cannot exercise self-control, they should marry. For it is
better to marry than to be aflame with passion." (I Cor. 7:8-
9.) " Now concerning the unmarried, I have no command of
the Lord, but I give my opinion as one who by the Lord's
mercy is trustworthy. I think that in view of the impending
distress it is well for a person to remain as he is. Are you
bound to a wife? Do not seek to be free. Are you free from a
wife? Do not seek marriage. But if you marry, you do not sin,
and if a girl marries she does not sin. Yet those who marry
will have worldly troubles, and I would spare you that. . . .
I want you to be free from anxieties. The unmarried man is
anxious about the affairs of the Lord, how to please the Lord;
but the married man is anxious about worldly affairs, how to

please his wife, and his interests are divided. And the unmarried woman or girl is anxious about the affairs of the Lord, how to be holy in body and spirit; but the married woman is anxious about worldly affairs, how to please her husband. . . . If any one thinks that he is not behaving properly toward his betrothed, if his passions are strong, and it has to be, let him do as he wishes: let them marry — it is no sin. But whoever is firmly established in his heart, being under no necessity but having his desire under control, and has determined this in his heart, to keep her as his betrothed, he will do well. So that he who marries his betrothed does well; and he who refrains from marriage will do better." (I Cor. 7:25-28, 32-34, 36-38.)

On the other hand, Paul said some positive things about marriage. For example: "The wife does not rule over her own body, but the husband does; likewise the husband does not rule over his own body, but the wife does. Do not refuse one another except perhaps by agreement for a season, that you may devote yourselves to prayer; but then come together again, lest Satan tempt you through lack of self-control." (I Cor. 7:4-5.) "Husbands, love your wives, as Christ loved the church and gave himself up for her." (Eph. 5:25.) "Even so husbands should love their wives as their own bodies. He who loves his wife loves himself." (Eph. 5:28.) Paul's magnificent description of love (I Cor., ch. 13) was not about the love of husband and wife but is certainly applicable to such love and is one of the most beautiful statements in all of literature.

That Jesus and Paul did not have identical attitudes toward marriage is reflected in their interpretations of the quotation from the book of Genesis: "Therefore a man leaves his father and mother and cleaves to his wife, and they become one flesh" (Gen. 2:24). Paul applies the statement to the relation of husband and wife. (Eph. 5:28-33.) But he also applies it to the relation between a man and a prostitute: "The body is not meant for immorality, but for the Lord, and the Lord for the body. . . . Do you not know that your bodies are members of Christ? Shall I therefore take the members of Christ and make them members of a prostitute? Never! Do you not know that he who joins himself to a prostitute becomes one body with her? For, as it is written, 'The two shall become one'" (I Cor. 6:13, 15-16). It is difficult to imagine Jesus subscribing to the latter usage. Such a relationship is the antithesis of oneness. It approaches the ultimate in the exploitation of a person as a thing. Jesus implied that husband and wife created a new spiritual entity. Apparently Paul did not see the relationship of the sexes on quite this level.

We must not conclude from what Paul wrote about marriage that he disapproved of it as an institution and would have done away with it if he could have done so. Each of his letters is addressed to a particular group of readers who lived under particular conditions and had particular problems. His primary concern was his readers' relationship to God and Christ. He was deeply disturbed lest the church be sidetracked by the events, affairs, and practices of the day, and thus not be prepared when the new anticipated era dawned. Part of what Paul said about marriage he said, in other ways, about other things necessary then and necessary now for the maintenance and continuance of life. For example, "The appointed time has grown very short; from now on, let those who have wives live as though they had none, and those who mourn as though they were not mourning, and those who rejoice as though they were not rejoicing, and those who buy as though they had no goods, and those who deal with the world as though they had no dealings with it. For the form of this world is passing away." (I Cor. 7:29-31.)

As it has rolled down through the centuries, Christianity has been like a growing snowball. In its passage through time and culture it has gathered to itself sticks and stones and odd bits of debris as well as pure white crystals of religious faith and thought. Not all the crystals have been of the same size and shape. Between the original teachings of Jesus and the interpretations of Paul and the complexities and varieties of present-day churches, there has been gathered together a massive accumulation of misconstruction and misunderstanding as well as insight and knowledge, arbitrary addition and omission as well as the slow and painstaking uncovering of historical evidence, assumption and wishful thinking as well as analysis and rationality, superstition as well as faith, cruelty as well as compassion, hate as well as love, crass materialism as well as lofty idealism. Each individual Christian must, himself, in the last analysis, reach his own conclusion, his own interpretation, as to what he will consider to be truth. In comparing the views of Jesus and Paul we find differences as well as similarities in detail. Even in comparing the Gospel records we find differences as well as similarities. The essential core of meaning of Jesus' life and teaching is something that the individual reaches only as he himself extends his faith beyond his knowledge, his hope beyond his information. Sometimes, in reaching a " Christian " point of view, individuals give more weight to other factors than to the life and teachings of Jesus himself.

VIII INTERFAITH MARRIAGE

THE PROBLEM

With increasing urbanization and its attendant breakdown of primary group controls in this country, with the decrease in the authority of the church, with the rapidly increasing number of young people attending colleges and universities, it is not surprising that the number of interfaith marriages is increasing. The last factor mentioned, namely, the college and university situation, plays a part because typically on the campus there are to be found a large number of young people of marriageable age separated from their backgrounds. This makes it possible for them to get acquainted through dating and to make judgments about each other on the basis largely of personal qualities without religion's being brought prominently into the picture. A significant proportion of these young people who become emotionally involved with each other are of different faiths. As they approach marriage they begin to raise questions concerning the advisability of an interfaith marriage. In some cases they are so emotionally involved that they decide to go ahead and marry in spite of difficulties that they cannot work out. In other cases they decide to stop going together or to break their engagement because they see in the interfaith marriage too great obstacles to success. In still other cases they face the problem squarely and intelligently and find that they have the personal resources to make an interfaith marriage succeed.

The problems of any interfaith marriage are relative. They are relative to the personalities involved, to their personal capacity for handling complex problems. Such marriages are also relative to the degree of meaning that the two persons attach to religion. An interfaith marriage would mean one thing to a couple who were only nominally church members; it would mean quite another to a couple who were very devout. Interfaith marriage is also relative to the degree of difference between the two persons' point of view. It would be one thing for, say, a Baptist and a Methodist, but quite another for a Jew and a Roman Catholic.

In an interfaith marriage a couple may become acutely aware of a fact that often escapes young people, namely, that marriage does not occur in a vacuum. It is not merely a matter of two persons being in love and living together as husband and wife. Interfaith marriage, like any marriage, occurs in a societal milieu. There are other people involved. There are other institutions involved. For example, there are typically two sets of parents who are interested in the new marriage and the children who may be born to it. The parents of each spouse are usually interested in having that person remain close to the parental family's practices, beliefs, and rituals. This interest is often intensified when grandchildren are born. In addition to parents there are friends, other relatives, clergymen, all of whom may be interested and some of whom may bring pressure to bear upon the young couple. Families visit and are visited. Grandchildren are accepted wholeheartedly, accepted reluctantly, or rejected. Parents either attend the wedding or they refuse to attend. They accept the child-in-law of different faith enthusiastically or at least graciously, or they may take every opportunity to snipe at the young couple and say, " I told you so."

The problem of having common friends is one that every couple must work out. In the interfaith marriage it is some-

times more than ordinarily difficult. This difficulty is intensified if the husband and wife attend different churches. It is
intensified further if they live in a community where there is
prejudice against a minority group to which one of them
belongs.

Many an interfaith couple can make a successful marital
adjustment together but find new difficulty when a child is
born. This poses the problem of the child's religious training
and eventual church affiliation. A small child can hardly be
trained in two faiths and attend two church schools simultaneously. A choice must be made. Which parent's church will be
favored? Some persons suggest that the solution for this dilemma is to let the child make his own choice when he is old
enough to do so. Granting that each individual should have
freedom of choice in this connection, to do it with a child, as
is often suggested, may be more easily said than done. It is in
a way like saying that the child will be left to choose his own
language, or his own mores and folkways, or the country of
which he will be a citizen. The child in his earlier years must
either be given some religious training, in which case he will
be biased; or he must be allowed to grow up without any religious training, in which case he will have an inadequate basis
upon which to make a choice. This statement is, of course,
oversimplified. Some couples do work out the problem by letting the child choose. Nonetheless, the problem involved in
doing so should not be underestimated.

FOCAL POINTS OF CONFLICT

Another complication to which some interfaith couples are
subject is what might be termed "focal points." Conflict is
normal in marriage. In all marriages there tend to be points of
tension and conflict — more, of course, in some marriages than
in others. These tensions and conflicts may be handled by the
couple successfully or unsuccessfully, constructively or de-
structively. When they are handled unsuccessfully, there may

emerge a general pattern of incompatibility of which there are numerous component and contributing elements. They often fasten on the more conspicuous elements, for example, sex, money, in-laws, and explain their marital difficulties in terms of these. One element that may readily be made such a focal point in a marriage is a religious difference. For instance, the couple may overlook the fact that their problems are being caused by a number of personality traits, situational factors, fatigue, pressures of various sorts, and feel that if they were only of the same faith things would be different. Or one spouse may go even farther and say, " If you were not a Catholic (or Jew or whatever it may be), our marriage wouldn't be in trouble."

Another point regarding conflict in marriage will bear emphasis. Some conflicts are resolvable; others are not at all, or not so readily, resolvable. For example, suppose a couple have conflict over money. There are several possible things they may do: increase income, decrease expenses, work out a new budget, learn the techniques of purchasing, make a new plan for apportioning responsibility for the use of income, and so on. But suppose a couple have conflict growing out of a conspicuous difference in age, or intelligence, or background, or religious faith. Such a conflict may not be resolvable at all or at best may be resolved wholly or partially only with considerable difficulty.

If interfaith marriage were only a matter of faith as the term implies, it would be one thing, and many couples who are now struggling with it might well be able to cope with it. But interfaith marriage usually also involves practice. This could involve things as varied as infant Baptism, Communion by drinking or by intinction, the eating of meat on Friday, the day of the week considered to be the Sabbath, the acceptance of divorce, the wearing of a sacred medal, kneeling or standing to pray during church service. Difference in practice, especially when accompanied by a degree of insistence or pressure on one side or the other, can lead to conflict.

CATHOLIC-PROTESTANT MARRIAGE

The problems of the interfaith marriage are often brought to their sharpest focus in the Roman Catholic-Protestant union. We must keep in mind, of course, that in any group there is a wide variety of personalities and great variation in the degree to which individuals adhere to the teachings of any church. There is also variation in the laxity or strictness with which clergymen interpret the tenets of a church. So when we discuss Catholic-Protestant marriage we are, of necessity, generalizing. The fact remains, however, that there is an official Catholic point of view, and this cannot be disregarded. It is reflected in part in the " Antenuptial Contract and Promises," which must be signed by both parties before a priest will perform the ceremony, and a priest must perform the ceremony to make it valid within the Catholic church. This contract is not uniform in all dioceses. One form of it is given below.

ANTENUPTIAL CONTRACT AND PROMISES

To be signed in duplicate in the presence of the priest by the parties entering a mixed marriage, and by two witnesses.

To Be Signed by the Non-Catholic Party
I, the undersigned, not a member of the Catholic Church, wishing to contract marriage with the Catholic party whose signature is also hereinafter affixed to this mutual agreement, being of sound mind and perfectly free, and only after understanding fully the import of my action, do hereby enter into this mutual agreement, understanding that the execution of this agreement and the promises therein contained are made in contemplation of and in consideration for the consent, marriage, and consequent change of status of the hereinafter mentioned Catholic party, and I, therefore, hereby agree:
1. That I will not interfere in the least with the free exercise of the Catholic party's religion;
2. That I will adhere to the doctrine of the sacred indissolubility of the marriage bond, so that I cannot contract a second marriage while my consort is still alive, even though a civil divorce may have been obtained;

3. That all the children, both boys and girls, that may be born of this union shall be baptized and educated solely in the faith of the Roman Catholic Church, even in the event of the death of my Catholic consort. In case of dispute, I furthermore hereby fully agree that the custody of all the children shall be given to such guardians as to assure the faithful execution of this covenant and promise;

4. That I will lead a married life in conformity with the Law of God and the teaching of the Catholic Church regarding birth control, realizing fully the attitude of the Catholic Church in this regard;

5. That no other marriage ceremony shall take place before or after this ceremony by the Catholic priest.

In testimony of which agreement, I do hereby solemnly swear that I will observe the above agreement and faithfully execute the promises therein contained, and do now affix my signature in approval thereof.

_____

Signature of the non-Catholic party

_____

Address

_____

City or Town

To Be Signed by the Catholic Party

I, the undersigned, a member of the Catholic Church, wishing to contract marriage with the non-Catholic party whose signature is affixed above to this mutual agreement, being of sound mind and perfectly free, and only after understanding fully the import of my action, do hereby enter into this mutual agreement, understanding that the execution of this agreement and the promises therein contained are made in contemplation of and in consideration for the consent, marriage, and consequent change of my status, and I, therefore, hereby agree:

1. That I shall have all my children, both boys and girls, that may be born of this union, baptized and educated solely in the faith of the Roman Catholic Church. I understand that in case of my death, or in the event of a dispute, the custody of all the children shall be given to such guardians as to assure the faithful execution of this covenant and promise;

2. That I will practice my Catholic religion faithfully and will strive, especially by example, prayer, and the frequentation of the Sacraments, to bring about the conversion of my consort;

3. That I will lead a married life in conformity with the Law of God and the teaching of the Catholic Church regarding birth control, realizing fully the attitude of the Catholic Church in this regard;
4. That no other marriage ceremony shall take place before or after this ceremony by the Catholic priest.

_____

Signature of the Catholic party

_____

Address

_____

City or Town

Signed in the presence of:

_____ _____
Witness *Witness*

I, the undersigned, do hereby attest that the parties whose signatures are affixed to the above agreement and promises appeared before me personally on the given date, and fully understanding the import and meaning of the aforementioned agreement and promises, freely entered into this agreement and signed the above in my presence.

_____

(Pastor — Assistant)

Date: _____

TWO COPIES of this form should be filled in and sent to the Chancery. One copy, when duly signed, dated and sealed by the Chancellor, will be returned to the priest to be kept in the parish archives; the other copy will be retained in the Chancery. See " Synodus Dioecesana Ludovici Septima — 1929 "
(Page 54 No. 95 under 2).

When this contract is examined objectively, and without implying criticism but only realism, it may be seen that the promises are one-sided in that the greater burden is placed upon the Protestant. The Catholic party agrees in general to do what he would do in any marriage, interfaith or otherwise. The Protestant party, with the exception of giving the other person religious freedom, agrees to things he would not do were he not entering an interfaith marriage.

These promises constitute a moral obligation. To pretend to make them without having the intention of keeping them would be to start a marriage with misrepresentation and deceit. The existence of the antenuptial contract and promises constitutes one of the major reasons for which the Catholic-Protestant marriage is difficult. This reason grows out of the fact that the couple, more especially the Protestant, make promises under one set of circumstances and are then expected to carry them out under another set of circumstances that were beyond their experience at the time the promises were made. For example, imagine a young couple in love. They are discussing marriage. Each admires as well as loves the other, and in so far as possible each wants to be generous and broadminded. In some respects this is easier for the Protestant because he is free from official expectation and pressure to which the Catholic is subject. The Protestant says something to this effect: " I love you and admire you. I don't know much about your church, but the fact that it is your church is good enough for me. After all, the important thing is to be a good Christian, not the church to which you belong. So I won't mind at all having our children trained in the Catholic church." It is one thing to say that about children yet unborn. It is quite another thing several years later to answer the questions of a child who is being taught things to which the Protestant parent cannot honestly subscribe in a church of which that parent is not a member and in the activities of which he cannot fully participate.

Let us go back to the young couple discussing marriage. Like most young couples, they want to have children. Like many, they want several. So, being in love and wanting very much to get married and have a family, it becomes easy for them to agree to let nature take its course, because they stand eagerly ready to accept all the children nature provides. So they find it relatively easy to agree to use no contraception. Several years pass. They now have three children, whom they love, but these children arrived in rapid succession. The wife's health has not been too good. The budget has been strained. Their home is too small. They really do not want any more children for a while, until they can "get on their feet." Now they are not so sure they want all the children nature can provide and at the rate at which she provides them. They would like from now on to space their children, to have them when they are ready for them. Being young and in love, they do not find it either desirable or possible to eliminate the sexual aspect of their marriage. The Protestant spouse would like to resort to contraception, but is conscience-stricken because of the antenuptial promise. The Catholic spouse is unalterably opposed to the use of any contraceptive by either spouse. What do they do? They did not foresee such a dilemma when they signed the antenuptial contract.

JEWISH–NON-JEWISH MARRIAGE

In the Jewish–non-Jewish marriage there is sometimes a problem of prejudice. This problem is not one-sided. Jews are as keenly and as often prejudiced against non-Jews as non-Jews are against Jews. Prejudice, no matter who feels it, is bad enough, but the prejudice of the majority group against the minority contains seeds of greater danger. Again the problem may be brought to a focus with the arrival of a child. How will the child be trained: as a Jew or as a Christian? Or will the child be given no religious training? Will the child be accepted by non-Jews or become the victim of prejudice? Young people of mixed parentage are sometimes torn by conflict. If they classify themselves as non-Jews because of one parent, they seem to themselves to be disloyal to the other parent in a way that suggests cowardice. If, on the other hand, they classify themselves as Jews, they subject themselves and their children to possible anti-Jewish prejudice.

When a child of mixed parentage is subjected to anti-Jewish prejudice, this fact may be extremely difficult for the non-Jewish parent to accept. Although they do not like it and are often deeply hurt by it, Jews are used to anti-Jewish prejudice in the sense that they learn to live with it. Non-Jews, on the other hand, belonging to the majority group, may know intellectually that some Jews have prejudice against them; but they are seldom the victim of it and it does not, therefore, involve their emotions. When a non-Jewish parent is confronted with discrimination against his child because of anti-Jewish prejudice, it may be more than he knows how to handle. Being a member of the majority group, he has taken his own aspirations and privileges for granted. He assumed that since his child had one non-Jewish parent, the child, too, would have the privileges of the majority group. Such a parent has not had the opportunity to learn to live with that type of prejudice. He is perhaps more deeply hurt when his child is discriminated against than if he himself were the victim.

Most readers of this book will be Protestant Christians. Because of this fact, it is easy for them to fall into the trap of assuming that Catholic-Protestant marriage is a Protestant problem and Jewish–non-Jewish marriage a problem only for non-Jews. It is well to remember, both in considering the problem in general and in working out a particular marriage, that the interfaith marriage is a two-sided problem, a problem just as complex for one spouse as for the other, no matter what their respective religious classifications.

Can Interfaith Marriage Succeed?

Up to this point we have painted a rather dark picture of interfaith marriage. We do not mean to imply that such marriage can never be worked out successfully. We know that it can. But to work it out successfully requires both the presence of personal resources on the part of the couple and the exertion of effort with understanding, since the interfaith marriage, by its very nature, may be expected to involve the problems and adjustments of ordinary marriage plus those which grow out of the religious difference.

One of the problems of interfaith marriage when the husband and wife attend different churches is their necessary deprivation of the contribution to their marital adjustment that comes from the participation in a common activity as potentially productive as church attendance. To circumvent this problem, some interfaith couples reach a compromise by which one attends the church of the other. Some couples choose to attend a third church, which is neither spouse's church. In some cases this is relatively easily accomplished. For example, a Baptist and a Methodist may agree to attend a Presbyterian church. In other cases, however, it is relatively difficult because there is no church that satisfies both. For example, for a Catholic and a Protestant there is no " in between " church. The same is true for a Jew and a Christian.

It goes almost without saying, that the more each spouse knows about the other's point of view, the better for their marriage adjustment. Such knowledge would not, of course, guarantee acceptance. It could not, in and of itself, prevent conflict. But knowing why an individual does as he does is often the first step toward accepting what he does. Hence, it would seem advisable for a young couple contemplating interfaith marriage to do what they can to become informed on each other's faith. This is sometimes more readily said than done. For example, a Protestant is freer to learn about the Catholic point of view than a Catholic is to learn about a particular Protestant point of view.

In addition to the above, it seems advisable for a young couple to talk over their contemplated marriage with both clergymen and with both sets of parents, if this can be done. Since such persons will be a very important part of the societal milieu in which their marriage occurs, it is to their advantage to begin to fit their marriage into the societal situation before the wedding.

Human spirituality or a spiritual relationship is something about which accurate judgment cannot be made readily. It does not depend upon expressed faith or upon church affiliation. It would, therefore, be the height of presumption to assert that in an interfaith marriage a couple cannot achieve that spiritual relationship which Jesus described as becoming one. But that it might be a more difficult achievement for a couple whose religious orientations were different and that a common orientation is a considerable asset in this process of becoming one, is a not unreasonable assumption. It may be that, as an old proverb says, " Many are the paths which lead in shadow up the side of the mountain; but from the cloudless summit all who climb behold the selfsame moon." Perhaps in the last analysis all religious orientations are of the same essence and directed toward the same ultimate point of focus. Nonetheless, for a couple to climb the mountain together, side by side on the same path, may well provide them with something that cannot be provided when they climb alone by different paths, even though their paths do lead toward the same summit.

APPENDIXES

A. PERTINENT VERSES FROM THE
NEW TESTAMENT

MATTHEW

5:27-32

" You have heard that it was said, ' You shall not commit adultery.' But I say to you that every one who looks at a woman lustfully has already committed adultery with her in his heart. If your right eye causes you to sin, pluck it out and throw it away; it is better that you lose one of your members than that your whole body be thrown into hell. And if your right hand causes you to sin, cut it off and throw it away; it is better that you lose one of your members than that your whole body go into hell.

" It was also said, ' Whoever divorces his wife, let him give her a certificate of divorce.' But I say to you that every one who divorces his wife, except on the ground of unchastity, makes her an adulteress; and whoever marries a divorced woman commits adultery."

15:10-11; 17-20

And he called the people to him and said to them, " Hear and understand: not what goes into the mouth defiles a man, but what comes out of the mouth, this defiles a man."

" Do you not see that whatever goes into the mouth passes into the stomach, and so passes on? But what comes out of the mouth proceeds from the heart, and this defiles a man. For out of the heart come evil thoughts, murder, adultery, fornication, theft, false witness, slander. These are what defile a man; but to eat with unwashed hands does not defile a man."

19:3-12

And Pharisees came up to him and tested him by asking, "Is it lawful to divorce one's wife for any cause?" He answered, "Have you not read that he who made them from the beginning made them male and female, and said, 'For this reason a man shall leave his father and mother and be joined to his wife, and the two shall become one'? So they are no longer two but one. What therefore God has joined together, let not man put asunder." They said to him, "Why then did Moses command one to give a certificate of divorce, and to put her away?" He said to them, "For your hardness of heart Moses allowed you to divorce your wives, but from the beginning it was not so. And I say to you: whoever divorces his wife, except for unchastity, and marries another, commits adultery."

The disciples said to him, "If such is the case of a man with his wife, it is not expedient to marry." But he said to them, "Not all men can receive this precept, but only those to whom it is given. For there are eunuchs who have been so from birth, and there are eunuchs who have been made eunuchs by men, and there are eunuchs who have made themselves eunuchs for the sake of the kingdom of heaven. He who is able to receive this, let him receive it."

MARK
7:18-23

"Do you not see that whatever goes into a man from outside cannot defile him, since it enters, not his heart but his stomach, and so passes on?" (Thus he declared all foods clean.) And he said, "What comes out of a man is what defiles a man. For from within, out of the heart of man, come evil thoughts, fornication, theft, murder, adultery, coveting, wickedness, deceit, licentiousness, envy, slander, pride, foolishness. All these evil things come from within, and they defile a man."

10:2-12

And Pharisees came up and in order to test him asked, "Is it lawful for a man to divorce his wife?" He answered them, "What did Moses command you?" They said, "Moses allowed a man to write a certificate of divorce, and to put her away." But Jesus said to them, "For your hardness of heart he wrote you this commandment. But from the beginning of creation, 'God made them male and female.' 'For this reason a man shall leave his father and mother and be joined to his wife, and the two shall become one.' So they are no longer two but one. What therefore God has joined together, let not man put asunder."

And in the house the disciples asked him again about this matter. And he said to them, "Whoever divorces his wife and marries another, commits adultery against her; and if she divorces her husband and marries another, she commits adultery."

12:18-25

And Sadducees came to him, who say that there is no resurrection; and they asked him a question, saying, "Teacher, Moses wrote for us that if a man's brother dies and leaves a wife, but leaves no child, the man must take the wife, and raise up children for his brother. There were seven brothers; the first took a wife, and when he died left no children; and the second took her, and died, leaving no children; and the third likewise; and the seven left no children. Last of all the woman also died. In the resurrection whose wife will she be? For the seven had her as wife."

Jesus said to them, "Is not this why you are wrong, that you know neither the scriptures nor the power of God? For when they rise from the dead, they neither marry nor are given in marriage, but are like angels in heaven."

LUKE
14:25-33

Now great multitudes accompanied him; and he turned and said to them, "If any one comes to me and does not hate his own father and mother and wife and children and brothers and sisters, yes, and even his own life, he cannot be my disciple. Whoever does not bear his own cross and come after me, cannot be my disciple. For which of you, desiring to build a tower, does not first sit down and count the cost, whether he has enough to complete it? Otherwise, when he has laid a foundation, and is not able to finish, all who see it begin to mock him, saying, ' This man began to build, and was not able to finish.' Or what king, going to encounter another king in war, will not sit down first and take counsel whether he is able with ten thousand to meet him who comes against him with twenty thousand? And if not, while the other is yet a great way off, he sends an embassy and asks terms of peace. So therefore, whoever of you does not renounce all that he has cannot be my disciple."

16:18

" Every one who divorces his wife and marries another commits adultery, and he who marries a woman divorced from her husband commits adultery."

20:27-38

There came to him some Sadducees, those who say that there is no resurrection, and they asked him a question, saying, " Teacher, Moses wrote for us that if a man's brother dies, having a wife but no children, the man must take the wife and raise up children for his brother. Now there were seven brothers; the first took a wife, and died without children; and the second and the third took her, and likewise all seven left no children and died. Afterward the woman also died. In the resurrection, therefore, whose wife will the woman be? For the seven had her as wife."

And Jesus said to them, "The sons of this age marry and are given in marriage; but those who are accounted worthy to attain to that age and to the resurrection from the dead neither marry nor are given in marriage, for they cannot die any more, because they are equal to angels and are sons of God, being sons of the resurrection. But that the dead are raised, even Moses showed, in the passage about the bush, where he calls the Lord the God of Abraham and the God of Isaac and the God of Jacob. Now he is not God of the dead, but of the living; for all live to him."

John
8:2-11

Early in the morning he came again to the temple; all the people came to him, and he sat down and taught them. The scribes and the Pharisees brought a woman who had been caught in adultery, and placing her in the midst they said to him, "Teacher, this woman has been caught in the act of adultery. Now in the law Moses commanded us to stone such. What do you say about her?" This they said to test him, that they might have some charge to bring against him. Jesus bent down and wrote with his finger on the ground. And as they continued to ask him, he stood up and said to them, "Let him who is without sin among you be the first to throw a stone at her." And once more he bent down and wrote with his finger on the ground. But when they heard it, they went away, one by one, beginning with the eldest, and Jesus was left alone with the woman standing before him. Jesus looked up and said to her, "Woman, where are they? Has no one condemned you?" She said, "No one, Lord." And Jesus said, "Neither do I condemn you; go, and do not sin again."

ROMANS
7:1-3

Do you not know, brethren — for I am speaking to those who know the law — that the law is binding on a person only during his life? Thus a married woman is bound by law to her husband as long as he lives; but if her husband dies she is discharged from the law concerning the husband. Accordingly, she will be called an adulteress if she lives with another man while her husband is alive. But if her husband dies she is free from that law, and if she marries another man she is not an adulteress.

I CORINTHIANS
5:1-2

It is actually reported that there is immorality among you, and of a kind that is not found even among pagans; for a man is living with his father's wife. And you are arrogant! Ought you not rather to mourn? Let him who has done this be removed from among you.

6:9 to 7:16

Do you not know that the unrighteous will not inherit the kingdom of God? Do not be deceived; neither the immoral, nor idolaters, nor adulterers, nor homosexuals, nor thieves, nor the greedy, nor drunkards, nor revilers, nor robbers will inherit the kingdom of God. And such were some of you. But you were washed, you were sanctified, you were justified in the name of the Lord Jesus Christ and in the Spirit of our God.

"All things are lawful for me," but not all things are helpful. "All things are lawful for me," but I will not be enslaved by anything. "Food is meant for the stomach and the stomach for food " — and God will destroy both one and the other. The body is not meant for immorality, but for the Lord, and the Lord for the body. And God raised the Lord and will also raise us up by his power. Do you not know that your bodies are members of Christ? Shall I therefore take the members of Christ and make them members of a prostitute? Never! Do you not know that he who joins himself to a prostitute becomes one body with her? For, as it is written, " The two shall become one." But he who is united to the Lord becomes one spirit with him. Shun immorality. Every other sin which a man commits is outside the body; but the immoral man sins against his own body. Do you not know that your body is a temple of the Holy Spirit within you, which you have from God? You are not your own; you were bought with a price. So glorify God in your body.

Now concerning the matters about which you wrote. It is well for a man not to touch a woman. But because of the temptation to immorality, each man should have his own wife and each woman her own husband. The husband should give to his wife her conjugal rights, and likewise the wife to her husband. For the wife does not rule over her own body, but the husband does; likewise the husband does not rule over his own body, but the wife does. Do not refuse one another except perhaps by agreement for a season, that you may devote yourselves to prayer; but then come together again, lest Satan tempt you through lack of self-control. I say this by way of concession, not of command. I wish that all were as I myself am. But each has his own special gift from God, one of one kind and one of another.

To the unmarried and the widows I say that it is well for them to remain single as I do. But if they cannot exercise self-control, they should marry. For it is better to marry than to be aflame with passion.

To the married I give charge, not I but the Lord, that

the wife should not separate from her husband (but if she does, let her remain single or else be reconciled to her husband) — and that the husband should not divorce his wife.

To the rest I say, not the Lord, that if any brother has a wife who is an unbeliever, and she consents to live with him, he should not divorce her. If any woman has a husband who is an unbeliever, and he consents to live with her, she should not divorce him. For the unbelieving husband is consecrated through his wife, and the unbelieving wife is consecrated through her husband. Otherwise, your children would be unclean, but as it is they are holy. But if the unbelieving partner desires to separate, let it be so; in such a case the brother or sister is not bound. For God has called us to peace. Wife, how do you know whether you will save your husband? Husband, how do you know whether you will save your wife?

7:25-40

Now concerning the unmarried, I have no command of the Lord, but I give my opinion as one who by the Lord's mercy is trustworthy. I think that in view of the impending distress it is well for a person to remain as he is. Are you bound to a wife? Do not seek to be free. Are you free from a wife? Do not seek marriage. But if you marry, you do not sin, and if a girl marries she does not sin. Yet those who marry will have worldly troubles, and I would spare you that. I mean, brethren, the appointed time has grown very short; from now on, let those who have wives live as though they had none, and those who mourn as though they were not mourning, and those who rejoice as though they were not rejoicing, and those who buy as though they had no goods, and those who deal with the world as though they had no dealings with it. For the form of this world is passing away.

I want you to be free from anxieties. The unmarried

man is anxious about the affairs of the Lord, how to please
the Lord; but the married man is anxious about worldly
affairs, how to please his wife, and his interests are divided. And the unmarried woman or girl is anxious about
the affairs of the Lord, how to be holy in body and spirit;
but the married woman is anxious about worldly affairs,
how to please her husband. I say this for your own bene-
fit, not to lay any restraint upon you, but to promote good
order and to secure your undivided devotion to the Lord.

If any one thinks that he is not behaving properly
toward his betrothed, if his passions are strong, and it
has to be, let him do as he wishes: let them marry — it is
no sin. But whoever is firmly established in his heart, being under no necessity but having his desire under control,
and has determined this in his heart, to keep her as his
betrothed, he will do well. So that he who marries his betrothed does well; and he who refrains from marriage will
do better.

A wife is bound to her husband as long as he lives. If
the husband dies, she is free to be married to whom she
wishes, only in the Lord. But in my judgment she is hap-
pier if she remains as she is. And I think that I have the
Spirit of God.

9:3-5

This is my defense to those who would examine me. Do
we not have the right to our food and drink? Do we not
have the right to be accompanied by a wife, as the other
apostles and the brothers of the Lord and Cephas?

11:2-16

I commend you because you remember me in everything and maintain the traditions even as I have delivered
them to you. But I want you to understand that the head
of every man is Christ, the head of a woman is her husband, and the head of Christ is God. Any man who prays
or prophesies with his head covered dishonors his head,

but any woman who prays or prophesies with her head unveiled dishonors her head — it is the same as if her head were shaven. For if a woman will not veil herself, then she should cut off her hair; but if it is disgraceful for a woman to be shorn or shaven, let her wear a veil. For a man ought not to cover his head, since he is the image and glory of God; but woman is the glory of man. (For man was not made from woman, but woman from man. Neither was man created for woman, but woman for man.) That is why a woman ought to have a veil on her head, because of the angels. (Nevertheless, in the Lord woman is not independent of man nor man of woman; for as woman was made from man, so man is now born of woman. And all things are from God.) Judge for yourselves; is it proper for a woman to pray to God with her head uncovered? Does not nature itself teach you that for a man to wear long hair is degrading to him, but if a woman has long hair, it is her pride? For her hair is given to her for a covering. If any one is disposed to be contentious, we recognize no other practice, nor do the churches of God.

Ch. 13

If I speak in the tongues of men and of angels, but have not love, I am a noisy gong or a clanging cymbal. And if I have prophetic powers, and understand all mysteries and all knowledge, and if I have all faith, so as to remove mountains, but have not love, I am nothing. If I give away all I have, and if I deliver my body to be burned, but have not love, I gain nothing.

Love is patient and kind; love is not jealous or boastful; it is not arrogant or rude. Love does not insist on its own way; it is not irritable or resentful; it does not rejoice at wrong, but rejoices in the right. Love bears all things, believes all things, hopes all things, endures all things.

Love never ends; as for prophecy, it will pass away; as

for tongues, they will cease; as for knowledge, it will pass away. For our knowledge is imperfect and our prophecy is imperfect; but when the perfect comes, the imperfect will pass away. When I was a child, I spoke like a child, I thought like a child, I reasoned like a child; when I became a man, I gave up childish ways. For now we see in a mirror dimly, but then face to face. Now I know in part; then I shall understand fully, even as I have been fully understood. So faith, hope, love abide, these three; but the greatest of these is love.

14:33-36

For God is not a God of confusion but of peace.

As in all the churches of the saints, the women should keep silence in the churches. For they are not permitted to speak, but should be subordinate, as even the law says. If there is anything they desire to know, let them ask their husbands at home. For it is shameful for a woman to speak in church. What! Did the word of God originate with you, or are you the only ones it has reached?

II CORINTHIANS
6:14

Do not be mismated with unbelievers. For what partnership have righteousness and iniquity? Or what fellowship has light with darkness?

EPHESIANS
5:21-33

Be subject to one another out of reverence for Christ. Wives, be subject to your husbands, as to the Lord. For the husband is the head of the wife as Christ is the head of the church, his body, and is himself its Savior. As the church is subject to Christ, so let wives also be subject in everything to their husbands. Husbands, love your wives, as Christ loved the church and gave himself up for her, that he might sanctify her, having cleansed her by the washing of water with the word, that the church might be presented before him in splendor, without spot or wrinkle or any such thing, that she might be holy and without blemish. Even so husbands should love their wives as their own bodies. He who loves his wife loves himself. For no man ever hates his own flesh, but nourishes and cherishes it, as Christ does the church, because we are members of his body. "For this reason a man shall leave his father and mother and be joined to his wife, and the two shall become one." This is a great mystery, and I take it to mean Christ and the church; however, let each one of you love his wife as himself, and let the wife see that she respects her husband.

COLOSSIANS
   3:18-19

Wives, be subject to your husbands, as is fitting in the Lord. Husbands, love your wives, and do not be harsh with them.

I THESSALONIANS
   4:1-6

Finally, brethren, we beseech and exhort you in the Lord Jesus, that as you learned from us how you ought to live and to please God, just as you are doing, you do so more and more. For you know what instructions we gave you through the Lord Jesus. For this is the will of God, your sanctification: that you abstain from immorality; that each one of you know how to take a wife for himself in holiness and honor, not in the passion of lust like heathen who do not know God; that no man transgress, and wrong his brother in this matter, because the Lord is an avenger in all these things, as we solemnly forewarned you.

I Timothy
    2:8 to 3:13

I desire then that in every place the men should pray, lifting holy hands without anger or quarreling; also that women should adorn themselves modestly and sensibly in seemly apparel, not with braided hair or gold or pearls or costly attire but by good deeds, as befits women who profess religion. Let a woman learn in silence with all submissiveness. I permit no woman to teach or to have authority over men; she is to keep silent. For Adam was formed first, then Eve; and Adam was not deceived, but the woman was deceived and became a transgressor. Yet woman will be saved through bearing children, if she continues in faith and love and holiness, with modesty.

The saying is sure: If anyone aspires to the office of bishop, he desires a noble task. Now a bishop must be above reproach, married only once, temperate, sensible, dignified, hospitable, an apt teacher, no drunkard, not violent but gentle, not quarrelsome, and no lover of money. He must manage his own household well, keeping his children submissive and respectful in every way; for if a man does not know how to manage his own household, how can he care for God's church? He must not be a recent convert, or he may be puffed up with conceit and fall into the condemnation of the devil; moreover he must be well thought of by outsiders, or he may fall into reproach and the snare of the devil.

Deacons likewise must be serious, not double-tongued, not addicted to much wine, not greedy for gain; they must hold the mystery of the faith with a clear conscience. And let them also be tested first; then if they prove themselves blameless let them serve as deacons. The women likewise must be serious, no slanderers, but temperate, faithful in all things. Let deacons be married only once, and let them manage their children and their households well; for those who serve well as deacons gain a good standing for them-

selves and also great confidence in the faith which is in
Christ Jesus.

4:1-5

Now the Spirit expressly says that in later times some
will depart from the faith by giving heed to deceitful
spirits and doctrines of demons, through the pretensions
of liars whose consciences are seared, who forbid marriage and enjoin abstinence from foods which God created
to be received with thanksgiving by those who believe and
know the truth. For everything created by God is good,
and nothing is to be rejected if it is received with thanksgiving; for then it is consecrated by the word of God and
prayer.

5:1-16

Do not rebuke an older man but exhort him as you
would a father; treat younger men like brothers, older
women like mothers, younger women like sisters, in all
purity.

Honor widows who are real widows. If a widow has
children or grandchildren, let them first learn their religious duty to their own family and make some return
to their parents; for this is acceptable in the sight of God.
She who is a real widow, and is left all alone, has set her
hope on God and continues in supplications and prayers
night and day; whereas she who is self-indulgent is dead
even while she lives. Command this, so that they may be
without reproach. If any one does not provide for his relatives, and especially for his own family, he has disowned
the faith and is worse than an unbeliever.

Let no one be enrolled as a widow who is under sixty
years of age, or who has been married more than once;
and she must be well attested for her good deeds, as one
who has brought up children, shown hospitality, washed
the feet of the saints, relieved the afflicted, and devoted
herself to doing good in every way. But refuse to enrol

younger widows; for when they grow wanton against Christ they desire to marry, and so they incur condemnation for having violated their first pledge. Besides that, they learn to be idlers, gadding about from house to house, and not only idlers but gossips and busybodies, saying what they should not. So I would have younger widows marry, bear children, rule their households, and give the enemy no occasion to revile us. For some have already strayed after Satan. If any believing woman has relatives who are widows, let her assist them; let the church not be burdened, so that it may assist those who are real widows.

TITUS

1:5-6

This is why I left you in Crete, that you might amend what was defective, and appoint elders in every town as I directed you, men who are blameless, married only once, whose children are believers and not open to the charge of being profligate or insubordinate.

2:2-6

Bid the older men to be temperate, serious, sensible, sound in faith, in love, and in steadfastness. Bid the older women likewise to be reverent in behavior, not to be slanderers or slaves to drink; they are to teach what is good, and so train the young women to love their husbands and children, to be sensible, chaste, domestic, kind, and submissive to their husbands, that the word of God may not be discredited. Likewise urge the younger men to control themselves.

HEBREWS

13:4

Let marriage be held in honor among all, and let the marriage bed be undefiled; for God will judge the immoral and adulterous.

I PETER
   3:1-7

Likewise you wives, be submissive to your husbands, so that some, though they do not obey the word, may be won without a word by the behavior of their wives, when they see your reverent and chaste behavior. Let not yours be the outward adorning with braiding of hair, decoration of gold, and wearing of robes, but let it be the hidden person of the heart with the imperishable jewel of a gentle and quiet spirit, which in God's sight is very precious. So once the holy women who hoped in God used to adorn themselves and were submissive to their husbands, as Sarah obeyed Abraham, calling him lord. And you are now her children if you do right and let nothing terrify you.

Likewise you husbands, live considerately with your wives, bestowing honor on the woman as the weaker sex, since you are joint heirs of the grace of life, in order that your prayers may not be hindered.

B. QUESTIONS FOR DISCUSSION

I. THE NATURE OF SEX

1. If Jesus disapproved of adultery as strongly as his statements regarding divorce imply, why did he save the woman caught in the act of adultery from punishment?

2. What is the significance of the statement that sex is a means of communication? How do we communicate in other than verbal ways? Are there any significant examples of non-verbal communication to be found in Christianity and the church?

3. What do we mean when we say that the sexes are complementary? What is the difference between " complementary " and " supplementary "?

4. What do you consider wholesome, what unwholesome, attitudes toward sex in marriage?

II. The Nature of Marriage

1. What are the similarities and differences between romantic love and Christian love? Can love be romantic and Christian simultaneously?

2. In what specific ways in marriage may an individual express his love for God and his awareness of God's love for him?

3. What kind of person does one have to be in order to be able to love? Is there any kind of person who is incapable of love?

4. Is there any difference between being ready for marriage and being ready for Christian marriage?

5. What is the significance of the fact that each person lives in a "private world"? Is the idea of "private world" consistent or inconsistent with the commonly expressed idea that "no man is an island"?

6. In what specific ways may dynamic good will play a part in marriage?

7. Christianity assumes that permanent monogamous marriage is the most desirable form of marriage. In the light of this, how can you account for the fact that other forms of marriage, such as polygamy, have apparently functioned successfully?

8. What constitutes adequate preparation for marriage?

9. Is love alone sufficient basis for marriage? What else is needed?

10. Is it possible for an individual to be in love with two or more persons at the same time?

11. What are the similarities and differences between loving and being in love?

12. Could any two Christians of opposite sex work out a successful marriage just because they are Christians?

13. What are the reasons for which some persons make a poor choice of marriage partner: (*a*) as persons making the choice, (*b*) as persons chosen?

14. There is a common saying that "the family that prays together stays together." Is this saying valid?

15. What would you expect two Christian spouses to do to contribute to the success of marriage that you would not expect two non-Christian spouses to do?

III. PREMARITAL SEXUAL RELATIONS

1. Assuming that a couple "draw the line" short of premarital sexual relations, on the basis of what criteria should they decide how far to permit their physical contact to go before the wedding?

2. On what basis should an individual decide what practices to accept and what to reject?

3. How should an individual make a decision as to what ought to be: (*a*) in his own behavior, (*b*) in society?

4. How much difference in degree of physical contact is appropriate in an engaged couple as compared to an unengaged couple?

5. What are the arguments for and against petting? What is a workable definition of petting?

6. What are the arguments for and against a "double standard of morals"?

7. Is it possible for a person to treat sex casually, even promiscuously, before the wedding and then work out marriage successfully?

8. Is there any difference between an unmarried couple who are in their late teens or early twenties and who hope someday to marry but not necessarily each other and a middle-aged couple who expect to remain permanently unmarried so far as sexual relations are concerned?

9. What, in your judgment, is the strongest argument against premarital sexual relations?

10. If an individual has had premarital sexual relations with someone other than the person he has married or expects to marry, should he tell that person?

IV. The Christian Wedding Ceremony

1. A man expects to dominate his wife, to be " head of the house," to " have the last word." Is such a point of view consistent with Christian teaching?

2. What is the difference between ego surrender and being dominated by one's spouse?

3. Since conflict in marriage is normal, what is the best way to handle it?

4. Specifically, what is meant by a redemptive experience?

5. Is a honeymoon necessary for the success of marriage? What contribution may a honeymoon make to the success or failure of marriage?

6. What is the difference between accepting another person and tolerating that person? Is acceptance possible without complete understanding?

7. At which points in the wedding ceremony would an immature person be least able to " measure up "?

8. What should a couple do if their parents object to their marrying?

9. Suppose a couple marry and then find themselves not getting along happily; what can or should they do about it?

10. Suppose a couple marry and then one discovers that the other is not the kind of person he was thought to be; what can or should they do about it?

11. Should a clergyman perform a wedding ceremony for any couple that ask him to do so? On what basis should he refuse such a request?

V. Jesus' Teachings

1. If Jesus' teachings are valid in part because he described man's true nature, how does it happen that people can disregard his teachings and apparently live happily?

2. How important is it to seek to reconcile all the apparent discrepancies in the New Testament? Can the New Testament

be a valid guide to Christian living even though it contains discrepancies?

3. Does the Bible have to be accepted on an " all or none " basis or is it possible for a person to accept certain parts but not others and still be a Christian? Are there any parts of the Bible that a person must accept to be a Christian?

VI. JESUS AND DIVORCE

1. Both the law and the church recognize that, for one reason or another under certain circumstances, a couple do not have the capacity to establish a marriage, even though they have a license and go through a wedding ceremony. Such " marriages " may be annulled. What is the similarity or difference between this and recognizing some time after the wedding that they have not had the capacity to establish a true marriage, even though they have a legal one, and then permitting them to divorce?

2. If a uniform divorce law were passed in all states, what grounds for divorce should such a law set up?

3. Should all states recognize incompatibility as a ground for divorce?

4. What would be the advantages and disadvantages of prohibiting all divorce and establishing legal separation as a substitute for divorce?

5. To what degree is divorce detrimental to children as compared to the degree to which serious marital conflict is detrimental to children?

6. Is it possible for children to be benefited by their parents' getting a divorce?

7. You are the chairman of a committee of a leading community organization. The committee's assignment is to formulate a marriage and divorce law that the organization will seek to have passed by the state legislature. What would you include in such a law?

8. What are the arguments pro and con as to whether remarriage after divorce is adultery or similar to adultery?

9. So far as a concept of adultery is concerned, what is the difference, if any, between remarriage after divorce and remarriage after the death of the marriage partner?

10. Is it possible for a Christian to reconcile taking the initiative in seeking a divorce with Matt. 5:38-48?

VII. Jesus and Paul

1. Are the sexes equal? Should they have identical, equal, equivalent, or unequal rights and privileges?

2. Why is it that more women than men are to some degree dissatisfied with their sexual classification? What might be done about this? If a particular wife were discontent with being a woman and assuming a woman's role in marriage and in life, how might the husband help her? How might he accentuate the problem?

3. Is woman's status higher or lower in this country today as compared to the past? What evidence do you have for your answer? What is likely to happen in the future? If women continue to get more rights and privileges, what is the result likely to be?

4. Do men want women to be equal to them? Do women want to be equal to men? What do the sexes expect of each other?

5. Should women strive to be as nearly like men as possible or as different from men as possible? What should a woman's objective in life be? Do you agree with the statement that " a woman's place is in the home "?

6. What suggestions can you make to improve the relationships between men and women in present-day U.S.A.?

7. What suggestions can you make to improve the education of the sexes in present-day U.S.A.?

8. A wife wants to be a wage earner but her husband objects. He gives as the basis for his objection some of the com-

mon arguments used by men under such circumstances. What suggestions would you give the husband? the wife? Who should determine whether or not a wife should be a wage earner?

VIII. Interfaith Marriage

1. Think of an instance of interfaith marriage with which you are familiar. What factors, attitudes, behavior, points of view, and so on have played a part in making it succeed or fail as the case may be?

2. How much difference in standards, values, ideals, attitudes, behavior, could a couple exhibit and yet work out a successful marriage?

3. To what degree and under what circumstances can the problems of interfaith marriage be solved by one spouse's joining the other's church?

C. SELECTED REFERENCES FOR FURTHER READING

Bailey, Derrick S., *The Mystery of Love and Marriage.* Harper & Brothers, 1952. Written primarily for Anglicans. A penetrating but somewhat technical analysis of the Christian point of view on sex, love, marriage, divorce, remarriage, " one flesh."

Bainton, Roland H., *What Christianity Says About Sex, Love, and Marriage.* Association Press, 1957. Chapters on " Fundamentals of Marriage in the Christian Church," " The Church on Sex and Marriage in the Period of the Roman Empire," " Christian Marriage Relations in the Middle Ages," " The Reformation on Sex and Marriage," " Puritanism and the Modern Period." This book is a revision of a chapter of Simon Doniger (editor), *Sex and Religion Today.*

Bayne, Stephen F., Jr., *Christian Living.* The Seabury Press, Inc., 1957. A discussion of " what most Christians agree that they should think and do." Includes a consideration of Christian marriage and sex in marriage.

Beach, Waldo, *Conscience on Campus*. Association Press, 1958. "An interpretation of Christian ethics for college life." One chapter is "The Morality of Romance." This book was "written out of the conviction that there are profoundly valid insights in Christianity for the dilemmas of college students. . . ."

Bertocci, Peter A., *The Human Venture in Sex, Love, and Marriage*. Association Press, 1949. A discussion of love, sex, and marriage in terms of comparative values. The approach is positive. Sex is discussed with relation to the whole of life and as an integral part of human experience.

Bossard, James H. S., and Boll, Eleanor Stoker, *One Marriage, Two Faiths*. The Ronald Press Company, 1957. An analysis of interfaith marriage by two sociologists.

Bowman, Henry A., *Marriage for Moderns*, 3d edition. McGraw-Hill Book Company, Inc., 1954. A text for college courses in preparation for marriage. Contains chapters on premarital problems, adjustment in marriage, mixed marriage, divorce, etc. Also contains a list of questions designed to assist in answering the question, How can I tell if it is really love?

The Church and the Law of Nullity of Marriage, S.P.C.K., London, 1955. The report of a commission appointed by the Archbishops of Canterbury and York. Contains a chapter on "The Nature of Marriage in Christian Doctrine."

Cirlot, Felix L., *Christ and Divorce*. Trafton Publishing Co., 1945. An interpretation of Jesus' teachings as strongly opposed to divorce and remarriage after divorce.

Cole, William Graham, *Sex in Christianity and Psychoanalysis*. Oxford University Press, 1955. A discussion of the ideas of Jesus, Paul, and later Christian thinkers as well as those of Freud and psychoanalysts.

Dentan, Robert C., *The Holy Scriptures*. The National Council, The Protestant Episcopal Church, 1950. A volume for laymen designed to be " useful in acquainting readers with the general position of contemporary Biblical scholarship."

Doniger, Simon (editor), *Sex and Religion Today*. Association Press, 1953. A compilation of articles on various aspects of the relation of Christianity and sex.

Duvall, Sylvanus M., *Men, Women, and Morals*. Association Press, 1952. An approach to sexual morality founded upon the conviction that " people have a right to sound guidance regarding sex conduct and standards, based upon the best scientific knowledge and the deepest insights available."

Epstein, Louis, *Sex Laws and Customs in Judaism*. Bloch Publishing Company, 1948. See especially the chapter on adultery.

Haw, Reginald, *The State of Matrimony*. S.P.C.K., London, 1952. An examination of the relationship between the teachings of the Church of England and the civil law relative to marriage and divorce since the Reformation.

Hiltner, Seward, *Sex Ethics and the Kinsey Reports*. Association Press, 1953. " It is the purpose of this book to examine the findings and methods of the Kinsey studies in the light of the Christian view of sex."

The Interpreter's Bible, Volume VII, Abingdon Press, 1951. This volume contains detailed analyses and commentaries on the books of Matthew and Mark as well as articles giving the background and history of New Testament writings in general.

Leach, William H. (editor), *The Cokesbury Marriage Manual*, 2d revised edition. Abingdon Press, 1945. Contains representative wedding ceremonies of several major Protestant churches, plus pronouncements of such churches on matters pertaining to marriage and family life.

Long, Edward LeRoy, Jr., *Conscience and Compromise*. The Westminster Press, 1954. " This is a book to help people to apply the demands of Christian faith to the decisions of everyday life."

Mace, David R., *Marriage: The Art of Lasting Love*. Doubleday & Co., Inc., 1952. The author says: " The title of the book expresses the emphasis I wish to make. In what I have written here I am concerned not so much with the scientific as with the artistic, aesthetic, emotional approach to marriage."

Mace, David R., *Whom God Hath Joined*. The Westminster Press, 1953. " In this book my purpose has been to relate what I believe about marriage in the light of the Christian faith. . . ." Presents Biblical verses, excerpts from other writings, the author's discussion for each of twenty-eight topics which constitute four weeks' daily readings.

Macmillan, Arthur Tarleton, *What Is Christian Marriage?* The Macmillan Company, 1944. Discusses the teachings and practices of the Church of England. There are chapters on marriage among the ancient Jews, the teachings of the Gospels and the Epistles on divorce and remarriage.

Phillips, J. B., *The Gospels Translated Into Modern English*. The Macmillan Company, 1952. A translation of the Gospels into language used in this country today.

Phillips, J. B., *Letters to Young Churches*. The Macmillan Company, 1947. A translation of New Testament Epistles into language used in this country today.

Phillips, J. B., *New Testament Christianity*. The Macmillan Company, 1956. An analysis of the Christianity of the New Testament and the nature and significance of Jesus.

Pike, James A., *If You Marry Outside Your Faith*. Harper & Brothers, 1954. A discussion of interfaith marriage.

Piper, Otto A., *The Christian Interpretation of Sex*. Charles Scribner's Sons, 1953. A discussion of the religious significance of sex.

Pittinger, W. Norman, *The Christian View of Sexual Behavior*. The Seabury Press, 1954. " A reaction to the Kinsey report."

Rosten, Leo (editor), *A Guide to the Religions of America*. Simon and Schuster, Inc., 1955. A compilation of articles, each written by a member of a particular denomination,

and answering such questions as "What is a Baptist?"
"What is a Catholic?" "What is a Christian Scientist?"
etc. Also contains many facts concerning church member-
ship, clergy, church schools, marriage and divorce.

Steiner, Richard M., *A Guide to a Good Marriage*. The Beacon
Press, Inc., 1955. A practical discussion written by a Protestant clergyman.

Thomas, George F., *Christian Ethics and Moral Philosophy*.
Charles Scribner's Sons, 1955. An interpretation of Christian ethics. Contains a chapter on sex and marriage.

Warner, Hugh C., *Divorce and Remarriage*. George Allen and
Unwin, Ltd., London, 1954. "What the Church believes
and why" as discussed by a canon of the Church of England.

Wedel, Theodore O., *The Christianity of Main Street*. The
Macmillan Company, 1951. An interpretation of Christianity for laymen, with the emphasis upon some of the
misconceptions of Christianity.

Williams, John Paul, *What Americans Believe and How They
Worship*. Harper & Brothers, 1952. A discussion of the
doctrines and practices of various churches in this country.

D. TALKS AND PANELS

Below are listed some topics for talks and panels. They are,
of course, only suggestions. They may be used separately, with
no particular relation to each other. Or there may be a series
of meetings, with topics arranged in some meaningful sequence.
But each meeting, though one in a series, should also be complete in itself since many persons will not attend the entire
series.

Topics may be used in any of the following ways:

1. A speaker discusses the topic. This is followed by audience
questions and discussions.

2. A speaker discusses the topic, to be followed by a panel
discussion, then audience participation.

3. There is a symposium, that is, a series of persons each of

whom makes a brief statement about the topic. After this there is audience participation.

4. A panel discusses the topic, this discussion to be followed by audience questions and discussion. A panel discussion is not just a helter-skelter talk fest. An effective panel discussion is both planned and channeled. This suggests preparation on the part of the panel members each of whom may be given an assignment in advance of the meeting. This assignment may consist of reading, formulation of questions, preparation of a brief statement on the topic. A good panel makes the planned portions of the discussion seem spontaneous, and the spontaneous remarks of members fit into the over-all plan of the panel. At the end of an effective panel the moderator, or some similar person, brings the discussion to a focus through a brief but meaningful summary. The panel is not just left " dangling in mid-air." A panel may also include a resource person, that is, an individual who has studied more thoroughly or had more experience in the area pertaining to the topic than is true of most panel members. In preparing for a panel it is also helpful for the members to get together before the actual discussion begins and have a " warming up " session in which they begin to discuss the topic and to hear what each member is going to emphasize.

In connection with any of the above plans, consider the following suggestions:

1. Relate the talk, the panel, the audience questions and discussion, to the content and emphasis of this book. If this is not done, the meeting may become just another session on the general topic of marriage and marriage preparation without a Christian emphasis.

2. If there is a problem of getting discussion started because the group is hesitant to talk, questions — even answers — may be " planted " in advance. Then at the appropriate time the people who have been given such questions will be ready to raise them to start discussion. This must not be done mechanically, however.

3. Interest may be stimulated through variety, using different methods in different meetings.

4. Films may be used as a point of departure for discussion and to stimulate interest.

5. If the group is large, " buzz sessions " may be effective. According to this plan, after a talk the group divides into several small " buzz groups," each of which independently discusses the speaker's topic and then after, say, fifteen to twenty minutes of discussion, reports to the entire group the high spots of what the " buzz group " has concluded.

6. It is helpful to have someone prepare a list of books related to the topic, or prepare a display of appropriate books that are available in the church, school, or public library. Sometimes the public library will co-operate in setting up a book display in the library building.

In summary, there are several things that will help make any meeting more effective:

1. Appropriate choice of topics — those which will meet the needs and interests of the group.

2. Careful advance preparation.

3. Assignment of specific responsibilities to a number of persons.

4. Group participation.

5. Use of resources such as resource persons, books, films.

6. Provision for variety in a series.

7. Focus — bringing each meeting to a focus.

Suggested Topics for Talks or Panels

" Male and Female He Created Them." Some of the more significant similarities and differences between men and women so far as attitudes and behavior are concerned. What needs to be done better to understand and adjust to these similarities and differences.

So You Want to Get Married. A discussion of the emphasis put upon romance rather than upon preparation for marriage. The qualities of a date as compared to those of a wife or husband. The difference between getting married and staying married.

A Husband on Your Budget. The problem of the wage-earning wife. The problems faced by college and university couples when the wife is working to help put the husband through school. How such problems may be met successfully.

It Is Better to Match than to Patch. The problem of choosing a marriage partner. What qualities are important in such a partner. Special problems of choice, for example, in cases where there is a difference of age, of religious faith.

What Holds Families Together. The family as an "area of participation." Freedom and responsibility. What draws family members together and what wedges them apart.

Must Families Feud? The relation of parents to children and children to parents. What can be done on either side to improve family living. Parent-child conflict. Problem children. Problem parents.

Dating — Know How or "No How"? What are acceptable standards in dating? What are Christian standards? How does Christianity apply to the relations between the sexes?

Making Marriage Meaningful. The factors contributing to success in marriage.

When Are You Ready for Marriage? A discussion of age and maturity. The relationship of young persons to their parental families so far as readiness for marriage is concerned. Marriage while in high school, college, university. Marriage in the light of military service.

How Can You Tell if It Is Really Love? A comparison of love and infatuation. Criteria for judgment. Traps and pitfalls.

Engagement as Marriage Insurance. The meaning and function of engagement. Common problems.

Boy Meets Girl — Then What? Standards of dating. Necking and petting. Going steady. Premarital sexual relations.

Test Pattern — How Much Distortion in Your Reception?
The family as a proving ground for maturity. What may
an individual do in his parental family to prepare him
for participation in his own future family?

Family and Church. The role of the church in family life.
The role of the family in church. How the church
unites the family. How the church may divide the family.
The pros and cons of the "family service" attended by
family members as a family. Religious education in the
home.

"With This Ring I Thee Wed." Analysis of the wedding
ceremony of a given church.

Is There Hope for the American Family? How family life
may be strengthened. Is the problem merely to lower
the divorce rate?

Marriage: A Christian Interpretation. A critique of this book.
Practical applications of Christianity to marriage.

E. USE OF FILMS

Appropriate motion pictures may be used either to introduce
or to supplement discussion on various topics. When such films
are to be used, the following suggestions will prove helpful:

1. The film should be considered as a tool to aid the discussion leader or panel. It should not be considered a substitute for the leader or panel.

2. The leader or panel members should preview the film to
be sure that it is appropriate for the discussion with which it
is to be used and also to become familiar with it. A film cannot be used effectively if the discussion leader or panel has
not seen the film before the group sees it.

3. After previewing the film, appropriate remarks concerning it and discussion questions based upon it should be formulated.

4. The film should be introduced to the group. This should

involve: (a) a brief discussion of the background factors and problems into which the film fits and to which it is directed; (b) suggestions as to what the group should look for in the film as it is shown; (c) a brief over-all resumé of the content of the film; (d) a few questions to keep in mind as the film is being seen.

5. After the film is shown, the leader or panel should let the discussion grow out of the film; but the discussion should not necessarily be limited to the film. It is more effective to give the group a few leading questions to start discussion than to have the leader say, " What do you think about it? "

6. After the discussion there should be a brief summary to bring the film and the discussion to a focus.

Each of the following films is 16mm. The name of the producer or distributor from which the film may be purchased is given in parentheses. At the end of the list the names and addresses of such sources are given in full. Many films may be rented or borrowed from local or state film libraries. A nationwide directory of such sources may be obtained from the Superintendent of Documents, Washington, D.C., for a small charge. The *Educational Film Guide*, published by the H. W. Wilson Co., New York, lists thousands of films and is available in many high school, college, or public libraries. State universities ordinarily have film catalogues available and also have films on hand that may be rented or borrowed. Typically there is considerable demand for such films, and arrangements for their use must be made far in advance.

Choosing for Happiness (McGraw; 14 minutes). Depicts the problems of a girl who defeats herself in dating because she evaluates boys too early in terms of " Is this the right one for me? " and also because she likes to manipulate others but sees no need for change in herself.

It Takes All Kinds (McGraw; 20 minutes). Shows how different personalities react to the same situations. The emphasis is upon wise choice of marriage partner.

This Charming Couple (McGraw; 19 minutes). Depicts a couple who, because of brief acquaintance, unrealistic attitudes, and a tendency to read into each other what is not there, confuse infatuation with love.

Marriage Today (McGraw; 22 minutes). Provides a look into some marriages through the eyes of the persons in them. These marriages are not perfect, but they have been made to work. The emphasis is positive and constructive.

Who's Boss (McGraw; 16 minutes). The problems of a couple, both of whom are wage earners.

Jealousy (McGraw; 16 minutes). A young wife's immaturity leads her to be jealous of her husband when there is no sound reason for it, but she misconstrues his behavior.

Who's Right (McGraw; 18 minutes). Depicts a young couple leading up to and engaging in a violent quarrel and raises questions as to factors contributing to their problem and possible solutions.

In Time of Trouble (McGraw; 14 minutes). A wife seeks her minister's help when her husband drinks. The situation in the home is shown. The minister sees that the wife also is at fault and he therefore tries to help the marriage by suggesting what the wife might do. The film raises a number of questions relative to marriage counseling.

Are You Ready for Marriage? (Coronet; 15 minutes). A young couple discuss their engagement and forthcoming marriage with a marriage counselor.

Choosing Your Marriage Partner (Coronet; 13 minutes). Depicts the problem of a young man trying to decide which of two girls to marry.

Courtship to Courthouse (McGraw; 15 minutes). One of the This Is America series. A presentation of the divorce problem in the United States in the late 1940's.

Families First (NY Com.; 17 minutes). Depicts the contrast between two middle-class families, in one of which there is harmony and in the other of which there is discord.

Going Steady (Coronet; 10 minutes). Explains going steady

as a normal step toward engagement but raises questions and problems for discussion.

How Do You Know It's Love? (Coronet; 12 minutes). Discusses factors to be considered in answering the question.

Marriage and Divorce (McGraw; 15 minutes). A survey of the problem of divorce and broken homes in this country as of the late 1940's.

Marriage Is a Partnership (Coronet; 15 minutes). Raises and discusses some of the problems that arise during the early years of marriage.

The Meaning of Engagement (Coronet; 13 minutes). Discusses the function of engagement.

SOURCES OF THE ABOVE FILMS

Coronet — Coronet Instructional Films, Coronet Building, Chicago 1, Illinois.

McGraw — McGraw-Hill Book Co., Text-Film Department, 330 West 42d St., New York City 36.

NY Com. — New York State Department of Commerce, 112 State Street, Albany 7, New York.